D1177576

WHAT JESUS SAYS

WHAT JESUS SAYS

The Master Teacher
and Life's Problems

ROBERT BOYD MUNGER

FLEMING H. REVELL COMPANY

To my Wife—

A constant companion, encouragement,
and inspiration in the things of Christ.

CONTENTS

INTRODUCING CHRIST'S INTERPRETER

AT PRINCETON SEMINARY, ROBERT B. MUNGER STOOD OUT AS one of the most spiritual and gentlemanly, most intellectual and promising of all the men I taught there. Since then, he has more than fulfilled all my expectations. As pastor of a large church beside one of the world's foremost universities, he has served as a winsome interpreter of the older orthodoxy. With "sweet reasonableness" he has commended New Testament Christianity to hosts of university folk and to countless other church-goers, young and old.

Dr. Munger has also been guide, counselor, and friend to many young people at conferences and elsewhere. By his love for human beings, one by one, his intellectual grasp of present-day problems, and his personal experience of transforming grace, he has commended the faith of our fathers to brilliant men of science, and to busy persons less scholarly. Many such reports have kept coming to me from friends on the Coast, whose judgment I value highly.

The title of this new book, *What Jesus Says*, appeals to me. At a time when so many of us "preach" mainly on a human level, and discuss Gospel truths negatively, this interpreter sends out this series of sermons, and in the right order. First, our Lord's teachings about Himself; second, His teachings about the reader and his problems today. First the doctrine and then the duty!

Even in the Athens of the West, the interpreter seems not

9

to fear his most brilliant hearers. Without camouflage or compromise, he sets forth doctrine and duty as they center in the Sinless Son of God. May his volume live up to its title, and fulfill all the hopes of his countless friends.

ANDREW W. BLACKWOOD

WHAT JESUS SAYS

THE MASTER TEACHER AND LIFE'S PROBLEMS

God, who at sundry times and in divers manners
spake in time past unto the fathers by the prophets,
Hath in these last days spoken unto us by his Son. . . .

Hebrews 1 : 1, 2

A SENTENCE FROM AN EDITORIAL IN "LIFE" MAGAZINE OF SEVeral years ago has remained with me. The article calls attention to the growing pessimism of current thought, the result, no doubt, of two disastrous world wars caused by the failure of modern science to solve the basic problems of life. It said, "People have become weary of the words of man. They have lost their confidence in man's ideas, man's programs, man's plans. They are hungry and eager to hear a voice from the other side—a voice of truth, a voice of authority whose ways will work in the lives of men. They are listening for a word from God." That word has been spoken. "God . . . hath in these last days spoken unto us by his Son, Jesus Christ" (*Hebrews 1:2*). It is in Christ that we find God's light for our lives. It is in Him that we discover the answer to our basic and fundamental needs, and it is in Him that we receive salvation.

13

Jesus Christ is the Master Teacher. His words bear Him witness. Critics set to catch Him for accusation are compelled to confess, "Never man spake like this man." The learned doctor, contrary to all his background, admits, ". . . Rabbi, we know that thou art a teacher come from God" (*John* 3:2). His Disciples who heard Him daily and knew Him well, are convinced. They cry "Lord, to whom shall we go? Thou hast the words of eternal life. And we believe and are sure that thou art the Christ, the Son of the living God" (*John* 6:68, 69).

Moreover, the words of Christ are contemporary facts. Whatever we may think about the origin of the gospels and their transmission, we have on the pages of the New Testament certain words attributed to Jesus. They bear witness to something unique and demand the attention of every self-respecting individual. That is to say, we must be honest enough to expose our minds to what Jesus is saying about life and about God. Before we dismiss the claims of Christ, we must listen to Him who claimed to be the Way, the Truth, and the Life. If He is the truest and highest we know, then we must not only sit at His feet and listen, but we must rise up and follow Him in the way.

It is the firm belief of the Christian that Jesus Christ is the revelation of God and that His teaching is eternal truth. He is more than an ordinary man, and He speaks with more than ordinary authority. You may have heard of the man who complained to his friends about his domestic difficulties. After listening to him for a while, the friend said, "Why do you let a mere woman push you around?" "Sir, replied the man, "I will have you know that there is nothing 'mere' about my wife!" There is nothing "mere" about Jesus Christ. He is not

14

an ordinary man. His words will bear witness that He is absolutely unique.

His words are unequaled in their timelessness and universal appeal. Two thousand years have passed since He taught beside the Sea of Galilee. Civilizations have come and gone. Empires have risen and fallen. Customs and traditions have known their ebb and flow. But the sayings of Jesus remain as pertinent, as applicable, as relevant as the latest book off the press. Other teachers have had their say and then stepped off the platform of history. No sooner has the echo of their voices died away than their teachings have become outmoded, outdated, and irrelevant. Not so with Jesus Christ. He is the Great Contemporary. We listen to the words that He spoke two thousand years ago, and we realize they are for us today. They have undying vitality. The only system of thought in the world which apparently has the power to meet and master dialectic materialism, to overcome and expose the falsehoods and pretensions of communism, is the truth which came from Jesus two millennia ago.

He speaks to all classes, all countries, all races, and all conditions of people. His words are treasured by those dwelling in the thatched huts of the African jungle or those living in the igloos of the Arctic, or in the apartments of American cities. His teaching enters into the homes of the poor and shares with them eternal riches. It breaks into the mansions of the wealthy and exposes spiritual poverty. Christ speaks a universal tongue, and everywhere, in every culture, men hear in Him the voice of the Great Contemporary.

The teachings of Christ combine profundity with simplicity, depth with clarity. The full scope of His truth always seems beyond us, and yet the heart of His thought is so simply expressed that a child can grasp it. With all the increase of knowledge in the world, no one has surpassed Him as the Great Teacher of life.

His parables, for example, are incomparable. Where in the pages of literature do we find jewels like "The Sower," or "The Good Samaritan," or "The Prodigal" and the father with open arms? Consider such words as these:

> Blessed are the poor in spirit: for theirs is the kingdom of heaven. Blessed are they that mourn, for they shall be comforted; Blessed are the meek: for they shall inherit the earth. Blessed are they which do hunger and thirst after righteousness: for they shall be filled. Blessed are the merciful: for they shall obtain mercy. Blessed are the pure in heart: for they shall see God. Blessed are the peacemakers: for they shall be called the children of God. Blessed are they which are persecuted for righteousness' sake: for theirs is the kingdom of heaven. Blessed are ye, when men shall revile you, and persecute you, and shall say all manner of evil against you falsely, for my sake. Rejoice, and be exceeding glad: for great is your reward in heaven. For so persecuted they the prophets which were before you (*Mat. 5:3–12*).

Or again:

> Therefore I say unto you, Take no thought for your life, what ye shall eat, or what ye shall drink; nor yet for your body, what ye shall put on. Is not the life more than meat, and the body than raiment? Behold the fowls of the air: for they sow not, neither do they reap, nor gather into barns; yet your heavenly Father feedeth them. Are

ye not much better than they? . . . And why take ye thought for raiment. Consider the lilies of the field how they grow; they toil not, neither do they spin: And yet I say unto you, That even Solomon in all his glory was not arrayed like one of these. Wherefore, if God so clothe the grass of the field, which to day is, and to morrow is cast into the oven, shall he not much more clothe you, O ye of little faith? Therefore, . . . seek ye first the kingdom of God and his righteousness; and all these things shall be added unto you" (*Mat. 6:25–30, 33*).

Or again:

After this manner therefore, pray ye: Our Father which art in heaven, hallowed be thy name. Thy kingdom come. Thy will be done in earth, as it is in heaven. Give us this day our daily bread. And forgive us our debts, as we forgive our debtors. And lead us not into temptation, but deliver us from evil: For thine is the kingdom and the power, and the glory, for ever. Amen" (*Mat. 6:9–13*).

His teaching is also unique in its authority. Without pretention or display, He calmly asserts that His words are final, His truth ultimate. "The words that I speak unto you, I speak not from myself but the Father abiding in me doeth his works." To the loyal Jew of Jesus' day, the words of the Mosaic law were the very words of God. There was no higher authority for them. Yet listen to the Master. "Ye have heard that it was said by them of old time, Thou shalt not kill . . . but I say unto you, that whosoever is angry with his brother shall be in danger of the judgment. . . . Ye have heard that it was said by them of old time, Thou shalt not commit adultery: but I say unto you, that whosover looketh on a woman to lust after her hath committed adultery with her already in his heart (*Mat. 5:21–22, 27, 28*). *I say unto you.* Jesus is the final authority. He does not labor His point. He does not argue His position. He does not buttress His authority. He simply states it. "And it came to pass, when Jesus had ended these sayings, the people were astonished at his doctrine: for he taught them as one having authority, and not as the scribes" (*Mat. 7:28, 29*). His teaching is self-authenticating; it is the truth, the solid stuff of reality. It confronts us with God.

The teaching of Christ is unique in its content as well. Some have ventured to say that there is nothing new in the teaching of Jesus; He simply said what others had said before Him. This is far from being established as a categorical fact. However, in the older ideas and concepts that He did restate, He poured into them such new light and gave them such new meaning and significance that He transformed them. What He has to say definitely sets Him off from merely human teachers.

Consider His teaching concerning God. He taught us things that the world did not know and had not been able to discover. As a matter of fact, almost the whole content of our knowledge of God in the Western world stems from what Jesus Christ taught concerning Him. He spoke of God as the living God, speaking, acting, loving in His world. Christ pulled aside the veil of speculation, enabling us to see our Heavenly Father—good and righteous, loving and forgiving, caring for all men, desiring that all should know Him and dwell together as brethren, children of the same Father.

Christ was absolutely sure about God. He was absolutely

certain about His character. He did not argue the existence of God, just as one does not argue the existence of the sun on a beautiful morning. Rather, we take the skeptic into the sunlight and say, "Here it is, streaming in glory all about you." So Christ leads us into the sunlight of the living God. In love and compassion He endeavors to open the eyes of those who will not see, to the most glorious and real fact of existence.

Moreover, Jesus speaks to us as One who knows all about God from the inside—as One standing on earth, yet speaking from the vantage of heaven. I am amazed as I study the gospels and read His words in this light. Jesus is not a scholar studying and pursuing truth. He is not a pilgrim on a quest to ascertain the nature of God. He is not seeking to know more about the Father or His will. He knows already. The eternal realities of God are already apprehended. Therefore, everything He says has about it a quality and viewpoint that is different. Horace Bushnell wrote long ago, "Jesus makes the world illumined with His words, fills it with an immediate and new sense of God which no one has been able to dispel."

What Christ said about Himself and about God, poses a problem. If you ask a man why he cannot believe in the deity of Jesus Christ, he will answer, "Well, my concept of God is so immense, so exalted, so spiritual that I cannot conceive of Him becoming incarnate and dwelling with man, being born in a manger, and dying on a cross." Who gave us this concept of God? Jesus, primarily.

Or another asserts, "I cannot believe in God, nor can I believe in Christ. There is too much pain and wickedness and suffering in this world. Can there be a God, much less a loving God, in a world like this?" We might ask, "Where did you get this idea of a good and loving God?" Primarily from Jesus.

Christ Himself raises the difficulty of belief in Himself. The greatest problem of faith in the deity of Christ is the deity of Christ. It is because of what He has told us about the nature of the Father that we have difficulty in accepting what He says about the nature of Himself. Suffice it to say, the profoundest, the purest, the most satisfying concept of God which we have comes from Jesus.

The Master Teacher has told us things about man which we never knew before and find nowhere else. He shows us the potential good in every man, the high and holy standard of God. He reveals to us the great gulf between what we are and what we ought to be and the grace of God which bridges that gulf and unites us to Himself. Only Christ has drawn near to man with the offer of personal fellowship with the Heavenly Father, calling him to brotherhood with his fellows in the family of God. Only Christ has given us moral absolutes for life. He said, "Be ye therefore perfect, even as your Father which is in heaven is perfect." He did not say, "Be approximately truthful, approximately loving, approximately pure." He said, "Be ye therefore perfect . . ."—an absolute standard of righteousness.

It is important to note this standard in the present day of relativism when morals are believed by many to be simply the product of the culture or the civilization. In certain tribes of Africa a man can have as many wives as he has cows with which to purchase them. In America, a man can have as many wives as he has money with which to divorce them. In one case it takes money to get them, and, in the other, it takes money to get rid of them—just a matter of the culture in which we are living.

Jesus says, "Be ye therefore perfect . . ." and He gives us a standard which is for all men everywhere and never changes. His words are a continuing challenge. "But I say unto you, Love your enemies, bless them that curse you, do good to them that hate you, and pray for them which despitefully use you, and persecute you; That ye may be the children of your Father which is in heaven . . ." (*Mat. 5:44, 45*). Beyond that we cannot go. Whatever the ethical variation of culture and experience, this call to love remains unshaken. Care for your enemy. Labor for his highest good and, if necessary, suffer for him, for this is God's way with man. One would think, as the centuries roll on, the words of the poet would be true. "Ancient good becomes uncouth," but not so! Christ's teaching is as far ahead of us in the twentieth century as it was ahead of those in the first century.

Jesus Christ is unique also in what He says about Himself. ". . . I am the light of the world: he that followeth me shall not walk in darkness, but shall have the light of life" (*John 8:12*). ". . . I am the bread of life: he that cometh to me shall never hunger; and he that believeth on me shall never thirst" (*John 6:35*). ". . . I am the resurrection, and the life: he that believeth in me, though he were dead, yet shall he live: And whosoever liveth and believeth in me shall never die . . ." (*John 11:25, 26*). What stupendous promises! What amazing claims!

"I and my Father are one" (*John 10:30*). "Come unto me all ye that labour and are heavy laden, and I will give you rest." (*Mat. 11:28*). "These things I have spoken unto you, that in me ye might have peace. In the world ye shall have tribulation; but be of good cheer; I have overcome the world" (*John 16:33*). "And I, if I be lifted up from the earth, will draw all men unto me" (*John 12:32*). "He that hath seen me hath seen the Father . . ." (*John 14*:9). What does one do with claims like these? Is Christ out of His mind? Is He deceiving us, or is He the Teacher of eternal truth?

Jesus Christ is unique also in that He embodied fully everything He taught. What He said by word, He lived out in deed. What He gave us in concept, He demonstrated in character. Of all the religious teachers who have walked among men, Jesus alone lived what He taught. Socrates and Plato held up their philosophies and said, "Consider these." Buddha and Mohammed enunciated their religious teachings and said "Follow these." Jesus simply said, "Follow me."

Other men have claimed to be divine. Abbe Effendi of Syria made claims to deity, but he did not live out the role. Men became disillusioned with him. But the life of Jesus fits the picture in all of its relationships—not only in His conscious, but in His unconscious attitudes.

When Dr. Norman Taylor of Mexico was working with a group of soldiers in an isolated post, he once gave a New Testament to an officer who knew nothing of Christ. He encouraged the officer to read the gospels and tell him when he returned in a few weeks just what he thought of Jesus Christ. Upon his return, the officer said to Dr. Taylor, "If there is a God in the universe, and if He came to earth and dwelt among men in order to save them, He would be like this man Jesus." Christ lives out the part. He is the Word become flesh. In this He is absolutely unique.

The Master Teacher is unique in that He empowers His pupils to obey His precepts. He does what no other teacher can do. He imparts the moral energy to fulfill the moral standard. He not only gives us the way we ought to go, but the will to walk in it. He not only gives us the truth, but He shares the life. He teaches us not only outwardly by words, but He teaches us inwardly by His own Holy Spirit. He gives us a new life inside, a new purpose, His own living presence. In this, of course, IIe is unrivaled.

WHAT JESUS SAYS ABOUT HIMSELF

I and my Father are one.

John 10:30

IN A REMOTE PROVINCE OF GALILEE AT THE HIGH POINT OF RO-
man power, there appeared a man dressed in peasant garb,
with the calloused hands of a laborer, who awakened unprece-
dented interest by His astonishing words and works. He was
a young man of about thirty years of age. He had only the
elementary school of the village synagogue. He had no political or financial backing. His itinerant ministry of teaching and
healing was of short duration—about three years—then He
was crucified at the hand of the religious and political au-
thorities who feared His growing popularity. Rather than
scattering His following, His death was followed by a movement of revolutionary impact and power. The effects of that
spiritual explosion remain a major factor in the world today,
the strongest influence for good and for God the world knows.

What do we think of this man Jesus? If He is not the Son of
God and Saviour of mankind, then let us get down to the bitter business of adjusting to a grim and hopeless world. If He
is, then let us give Him the full measure of our loyalty and

24

love. I believe He is indeed the incarnate Lord of glory. I would direct your thought to just one area of evidence—what Jesus thought and said of Himself.

He said things about Himself that no other man has ever dared to say. He made amazing, astounding claims to unique Being and absolute authority. He made these claims in a natural, sincere way and in complete humility.

Suppose we were to hear one say, "I am the way, the truth, and the life: no man cometh unto the Father but by me" (*John 14:6*). "I am the bread of life . . ." (*John 6:35*). "I am the light of the world: he that followeth me shall not walk in darkness, but shall have the light of life" (*John 8:12*). "I am the door: by me if any man enter in, he shall be saved, and shall go in and out, and find pasture" (*John 10:9*). "I am the resurrection and the life: he that believeth in me, though he were dead, yet shall he live" (*John 11:25*).

Think of what He said about Himself. Consider too, the kind of promises He made. He said, "Heaven and earth shall pass away: but my words shall not pass away" (*Mark 13:31*). "Whosoever drinketh of this water shall thirst again: but whosoever drinketh of the water that I shall give him shall never thirst; but the water that I shall give him shall be in him a well of water springing up into everlasting life" (*John 4:13, 14*). "Whatsoever ye shall ask in my name, that will I do, that the Father may be glorified in the Son" (*John 14:13*). "My sheep hear my voice, and I know them, and they follow me: and I give unto them eternal life and they shall never perish, neither shall any man pluck them out of my hand" (*John 10:27, 28*). ". . . All power is given unto me in heaven and in earth" (*Mat. 28:18*). ". . . and, lo, I am with you alway, even unto the end of the world." (*Mat. 28:20*).

Moreover, Jesus calmly places Himself above the greatest of mortals, above the most sacred of institutions, above the highest authority known to man. He says, ". . . a greater than Solomon is here" (*Luke 11:31*). He placed Himself above the temple, even above the Sabbath. "That the Son of man is Lord also of the sabbath" (*Luke 6:5*). "And I, if I be lifted up . . . will draw all men unto me" (*John 12:32*). What statements!

He dared to claim outright equality with God. "I and my Father are one" (*John 10:30*). They knew what He meant. They picked up stones to kill Him. In the fifth chapter of John's Gospel, there is a similar incident recorded. Jesus is by the pool of Bethesda. He looks with compassion upon a poor cripple who for thirty-eight years had lain helpless. He asks the unfortunate man if he really wants to be healed. The man gives reasons why he is not healed. Then the Master speaks, "Arise, take up thy bed, and walk" (*John 5:11*). At once he stands to his feet, take up his pallet and walks, rejoicing that he has been made whole.

Now the day on which this happens is the Sabbath Day and according to their tradition, no one is to carry so much as a stick on the Sabbath Day, let alone a mattress or a pallet. When the healed man is seen carrying his pallet, it arouses the fury of the religious leaders. They do not deny that a miracle has been performed and a ministry of mercy done, but it conflicts with the traditions of the fathers. They begin to accuse the Master of breaking the Sabbath law. In the last part of John 5:17 (RSV) we observe how our Lord replies. "My Father is working still and I am working." And for this reason ". . . the Jews sought all the more to kill him, because he not only broke the sabbath but also called God his Father, making himself equal with God" (*John 5:18, RSV*).

Some thoughtful student may call attention to the fact that most of the references just given are from John's Gospel, written particularly to present Jesus Christ as the Son of God. Perhaps these Scriptures are an expression of the later faith of the church rather than Jesus' own mind and message. But. we cannot separate these claims of Jesus from the gospel record. They are woven into its very fabric. They cannot be deleted from the story without demolishing the structure. It is rather difficult to manage an umbrella from which the spokes have been removed. Just try it sometime and see what happens! But neither will the gospel hold together without the strong spokes of these claims of Christ to uniqueness. If He did not make these claims, then we know nothing whatever about His life. For the fact that Jesus felt and talked like this is as good as any historical evidence that we possess.

Moreover, we find these statements made throughout the entire gospel witness. For example, let us turn to Matthew's Gospel. In Matthew 11:27, He says, "All things are delivered unto me of my Father: and no man knoweth the Son, but the Father; neither knoweth any man the Father, save the Son, and he to whomsoever the Son will reveal him." Thus He asserts that He is the solitary Mediator between the Father and man. Only as He discloses the nature of God, can He be known by mankind. As if that were not enough, He moves on to say, "Come unto me, all ye that labor and are heavy laden, and I will give you rest" (*Mat. 11:28*). He offers rest and peace to the heart. He speaks then as no other man has ever spoken.

Or consider His words in the Sermon on the Mount. "Not everyone that saith unto me, Lord, Lord, shall enter into the kingdom of heaven; but he that doeth the will of my Father. . . . Many will say to me in that day, Lord, Lord have we not

27

prophesied in thy name? and in they name have cast out devils? and in thy name done many wonderful works? And then will I profess unto them, I never knew you: depart from me, ye that work iniquity" (*Mat. 7:21–23*). Who is this man who sets Himself up as the very touchstone of life in the day of judgment and declares He will determine who shall enter into life and who shall not?

Observe Him as He stands under solemn oath before the High Priest on the night of His trial and crucifixion. The High Priest leans forward in a fury, shouting, "I adjure thee by the living God, that thou tell us whether thou be the Christ, the Son of God" (*Mat. 26:63*). Jesus answers, "Thou hast said . . ." (*Mat. 26:64*). You are right. That is who I am. ". . . I say unto you, Hereafter shall ye see the Son of man sitting on the right hand of power, and coming in the clouds of heaven" (*Mat. 26: 64*). "Then the high priest rent his clothes, saying, He hath spoken blasphemy . . ." (*Mat. 26:65*). And they delivered Him to be crucified.

Jesus never would have been crucified if He had not made claim to be the unique Son of God. Thus, our Lord by His own words, sets Himself in a class by Himself. How do we understand this? Was he demented? Was He deluded? Was He a deceiver of men? Or was He divine as He said He was? Perhaps Jesus was suffering from delusions of grandeur. Perhaps He imagined Himself to be someone He was not. Perhaps He was sincere but mistaken about Himself.

Recently I heard of a scientist who desired to make a lie-detector test in a mental institution. He found a patient suffering from delusions of grandeur who thought he was Napoleon Bonaparte. Showing the instrument to the man, the scientist said, "This is a lie-detector. I want you to tell me the truth." Then he adjusted the apparatus and asked, "Are you Napoleon Bonaparte?" "No sir, I am not," the man replied. But the lie-detector showed that he was lying. Perhaps Jesus was deluded about His deity. But could the clearest light we have on life, the truest, purest word on relationships in family, in society or with God, have come through a disturbed or deluded mind? Of course not. It is unthinkable.

Perhaps He was a deceiver. But if, in order to accomplish certain good ends for humanity, He encouraged His followers to believe that He was more than He really was, then we are faced with the problem of explaining how it is that the highest morality humanity possesses, the strongest support to truth and integrity the world knows comes from a faker and a fraud. Could He out of untruth have produced truth, and by lack of integrity could He have created integrity? That too, we must disregard as an impossibility.

C. S. Lewis puts it tersely:

> I am trying to prevent anyone from saying the really silly thing that people often say about Him; 'I'm ready to accept Jesus as a great moral teacher, but I don't accept His claim to be God.' That's the one thing we mustn't say. A man who was merely a man and said the sort of things Jesus said wouldn't be a great moral teacher. He'd either be a lunatic on a level with a man who says he's a poached egg—or else he'd be the devil of hell. You must take your choice. Either this man was, and is, the Son of God, or else a madman or something worse. You can shut Him up for a demon; or you can fall at His feet and call Him Lord and God. But don't let us come

with any patronizing nonsense about His being a great human teacher. He hasn't left that open to us.

I believe that Jesus is exactly who He says He is, the Son of God and the only Saviour of mankind.

These amazing claims are supported by His equally amazing life. Occasionally someone appears on the platform of history claiming to be divine. There is a man in Philadelphia today who gathers his angels about him in Harlem heavens. He says he is God Almighty incarnate in the world. But serious and sensitive minds reject this as preposterous. Yet no one is offended by the pretentions of Jesus to deity. For 1900 years these claims have been preached and published near and far. Thoughtful, earnest people have responded to them and have seen in Jesus a man of absolute worth and goodness. In other words, He maintains His staggering claims.

Then look at this fact. Jesus has a most remarkable modesty. His life is one of intense and consistent humility, deeper and truer than any humility we know. He maintains this humility and this modesty even while He is making these tremendous affirmations about Himself. For example, He says, "Come unto me, all ye that labour and are heavy laden . . ." (*Mat. 11: 28*). He assumes supernatural authority, and follows it with words like these, ". . . for I am meek and lowly . . ." (*Mat. 11: 29*). Yet in Him there is no inconsistency or contradiction. Even the severest critics of Jesus hesitate to accuse Him of being conceited or absurd. They may find many things about Jesus they don't like or they don't agree with, but you seldom hear anyone saying that Jesus is conceited or absurd. Even the person who rejects Jesus Christ as the Son of God does not

laugh at the idea of Christ being the Son of God, for Christ's
life supports His words.

Can you think of any other person in all history who could
seriously maintain the claim to be incarnate deity? Could
Plato or Aristotle or Caesar or the Emperor Hirohito or any
other figure of history? Could such a personality have been
imagined? Could Dante or Milton or Shakespeare have conceived such a character and supported its consistency through
even the shortest drama?

Horace Bushnell in his book, *The Character of Jesus,* writes:

> Take the range if you will, of all the great philosophers
> and saints, and choose out one that is most competent.
> Or if, perchance, some one of you may imagine that he is
> himself about upon a level with Jesus (as we hear that
> some of you do), let him come forward in this trial and
> say "Follow me"—"be worthy of me"—"I am the light of
> the world"—"Ye are from beneath, I am from above."—
> "Behold a greater than Solomon is here." Take on all
> these transcendent assumptions and see how soon your
> glory will be sifted out of you by the detective gaze, and
> darkened by the contempt of mankind! Why not? Is not
> the challenge fair? Do you not tell us that you can say as
> divine things as He? Is it not in you too, of course, to do
> what is human? Are you not in the front rank of human
> developments? Do you not rejoice in the power to rec-
> tify many mistakes and errors in the words of Jesus? Give
> us then this one experiment, and see if it does not prove
> to you a truth that is of some consequence; viz, that you
> are a man, and that Jesus Christ is more!

Finally, let me say that I believe in Jesus Christ because

what He said about Himself is supported not only by His life, but by what He thought. The role of deity in flesh is consistent to the center of conscious and subconscious response. To act like God and support the role by a thousand acts and attitudes is one thing, but to think and feel like God is quite another and equally amazing thing.

Consider these facts. Jesus of Nazareth disowns all repentance. He never acknowledges sin. He never expresses regret. He evidences no awareness of mistakes, no feelings of compunction. He does not sense a need to ask anyone for forgiveness. Now, human piety begins with repentance. We cannot conceive a truly devout person who does not acknowledge unworthiness before the perfection and holiness of God. The humility of the Master is without inward humiliation and in this He stands alone. The very breath of prayer is the seeking of forgiveness. No such prayer ever fell from the lips of Jesus. On the cross, He prayed, "Father, forgive them for they know not what they do" (*Luke 23:34*). He did not pray, "Father, forgive Me." In another, this would be arrogant self-righteousness. But in Jesus, it flowed out of a meek and lowly heart. He did not ask for forgiveness because He did not need forgiveness.

He is constantly aware of divine resources always available. His miracles are not preceded by long and strenuous intercessions or labored incantations. Simply and easily He speaks and the power of God is manifest. Pilate, the Roman Governor looks in amazement at this man standing before him in the Judgment Hall. He is the only One who is quiet and undisturbed in all the tumult of accusation that is raging against Him. The crowd shouts "Crucify him!" But He remains silent. So, the Governor, looking into the face of Jesus says, ". . .knowest thou not that I have power to crucify ... (*John 19:10*). And Jesus replies, "Thou couldest have no power at all against me, except it were given thee from above . . ." (*John 19:11*). He knows He is secure in the Father's will.

They come bearing word to Jairus, the ruler of the synagogue, that his daughter is dead. But Jesus enters into the room where the mourners are wailing and quietly speaks, ". . . the damsel is not dead but sleepeth" (*Mark 5:39*). They look at Him in amazement and contempt. Our Lord moves into the presence of death with the absolute confidence that at His word, the dead shall rise. He takes the hand of the little girl in His hand and speaks, ". . . Little girl, I say to you, arise" (*Mark 5:41, RSV*). And she lives! At all times He is conscious of omnipotent resources. This is unique. No one ever thought like that about himself. No one ever conceived such a character on the pages of any drama.

This divine self-consciousness is more fully seen in His dealing with sinners. Consider His word to the paralytic. ". . . Son, be of good cheer, thy sins be forgiven thee" (*Mat. 9:2*). This word is overheard by the Pharisees and the Scribes and they say within themselves, "Blasphemy! Who can forgive sins but God?" Jesus knows what they are thinking. He does not question their remarks. They were true. Who can forgive sins but God? Then with confidence, He speaks to the paralytic, "But that you may know that the Son of man has authority on earth to forgive sins . . . Rise, take up your bed and go home" (*Mat. 9:6, 7, RSV*). And he rises forgiven and healed.

Or again, listen to Jesus as He views the city of Jerusalem. Perhaps He is standing on the Mount of Olives, looking down upon the crowded city and the sun gleaming upon the white marble of the Temple. He cries out in grief, "O, Jerusalem . . .

how often would I have gathered thy children together, even as a hen gathereth her chickens under her wings, and ye would not" (*Mat. 23:37*). Why this outbreak of sorrow? Was it simply out of sympathy for the distress and darkness of the people of Jerusalem? No! The conflict in His soul was that He knew He had the power to save them and they would not receive Him.

Penetrate to the deepest level of the consciousness of Jesus of Nazareth and there is one consistent personality, fully man and fully God and a consciousness of being both at all times.

Jesus confidently assumes what is humanly impossible. He undertakes to do what no man, in the wildest flights of imagination, dares to attempt. He predicts the setting up of a universal kingdom. Contrary to the narrow and exclusive views of His time, He purposes to bring into being a kingdom of God, a new moral and spiritual creation of humanity for all peoples of all lands. He will restore mankind to the reign of God, to fellowship with the Father. He who never saw a map of the world, commands a handful of disciples who had never been a hundred miles from their homes, to go into all the world and teach all nations, bringing all peoples to God through His Name. Imagine a simple Galilean carpenter walking out of His shop to venture a scheme that dwarfs the grandest ambitions of Alexander the Great, to launch a plan of immense grandeur, scope, and purpose. His plan embraces all ages, reaching into all areas. Where did He get the confidence that His mission was going to succeed? He said, ". . . the gates of hell shall not prevail against it" (*Mat. 16:18*).

His expectation reaches beyond His death. In John's Gospel, we read of Mary and Martha ministering to Jesus. Mary takes an alabaster box of ointment and anoints Jesus for His burial.

Although He knows that before Him is the cross, He is not disturbed nor unsettled. Rather He says, "Verily I say unto you, wheresoever this gospel shall be preached in the whole world, there shall also this, that this woman hath done, be told for a memorial of her" (*Mat. 26:13*). Wherever the gospel shall go throughout the whole earth, what she has done will be remembered, He said. And two thousand years after this event, on the other side of the world, we are remembering what this woman did. Jesus was certain that His word and His work, His cause and His Kingdom would embrace the world and last forever.

Moreover He purposes to establish His reign and the Kingdom of God in a manner no human mind could conceive, not by force or compulsion, not by scepter or sword, not by crushing authority or a program of occupation, but by laying down His life. Whoever thought of such a thing! Whoever conceived that by dying an unjust death at the hand of enemies, one could establish a kingdom that would overcome the forces of evil and last forever? Jesus did! He said, "I am the good shepherd: the good shepherd giveth his life for the sheep" (*John 10:11*). "No man taketh it from me, but I lay it down of myself . . ." (*John 10:18*). ". . . the Son of man came not to be ministered unto, but to minister, and to give his life a ransom for many" (*Mat. 20:28*). "And I, if I be lifted up from the earth, will draw all men unto me" (*John 12:32*). He would win by love, through the giving of His life for them.

Napoleon once acknowledged, "Alexander, Caesar, Charlemagne and I have founded great empires, but upon what did these creations of our genius depend? Upon force! Jesus alone founded His empire upon love and to this very day millions would die for Him."

I believe that Jesus Christ is the Son of God because He talked like incarnate deity; He thought like it, He planned like it, He died like it, rising from the dead in glorious vindication of it. I believe in Christ because He evidences the divinity of His person today by bringing new life to those who receive Him. What do we think of this Man Jesus? Well, if you doubt what He says about Himself, ask Him to verify it in your own experience, surrendering to the truth He has to say about you.

WHAT JESUS SAYS ABOUT UNDERSTANDING OURSELVES

For the Son of man is come to seek and to save that which was lost.

Luke 19:10

I WONDER IF WE TRULY UNDERSTAND OURSELVES. I WONDER IF we have the answer to the basic questions of life. Who am I? What is my true nature? Why am I here? Where did I come from? Where am I going? What is the meaning of existence?

There is an immense amount of knowledge on almost every subject and in almost every field today, but we know very little about ourselves. I suppose the average American knows more about the operation of his automobile than he knows about the operation of his own heart. He knows more about the laws of the physical world around him than he does about the spiritual world within him. Psychologists claim that one of the basic conflicts in the human personality is the conflict between man and himself. He does not know how to adjust himself to himself. The noted psychiatrist, Dr. Carl Jung has written. "About one third of my cases are suffering from no

clinically definable neurosis but from the senselessness and
the emptiness of their lives. They do not understand themselves. They are unable to live happily with themselves." Says
a critic of one of Marquand's recent books, "He has all the
little answers; he does not ask the big questions." I rather
suspect that today we have the little answers, but few of us
are asking the big questions.

Jesus Christ comes to grips with the big questions of life. He
reaches down into the deepest hungers of the heart. He sheds
light into the hidden recesses of the soul. What is life? Why is
there suffering, evil, and death in the world? His answers to
these fundamental problems are satisfying; they fit all the facts
and embrace all of life's experiences. Christ tells us things
about ourselves which we cannot know apart from Him. In-
troducing us to our true selves, He sets up for us true stand-
ards and reveals our true worth as children of God. Disclosing
our true destiny, He gives us a revelation of life's true values.
He orients us to reality.

The Master teaches us that the meaning of existence is understood only in the light of God. This is our Father's world.
He has placed us on this earth and has a plan for us. His purpose is that we enter into fellowship with Him and share His
glory; that we do His will and dwell together as brethren.
Christ teaches us that man is not a coincidence, a sport of
chance who just happens to be here. We are creatures made
by the hand of God, capable of moral choices. Man is not
merely body and bulk, but a spiritual being created in the
image of God. He carries about him reflections of the Divine
Being in intelligence, the capacity for evaluation and judgment, and a moral sensitivity to right and wrong. He has ca-

pacity for fellowship with the most High. These are the principles about man that Christ sets forth.

The twentieth-century tragedy is that man is widely viewed as no more than a high-grade animal without ultimate significance or meaning. With this view current in our civilization, we cannot wonder that this century has seen a most humiliating degradation of human personality. Man is used as cannon fodder, the chattel of the all-powerful State, thrust into death factories for fertilizer. Many are living simply for animal appetites and creature comforts, scarcely lifting their eyes above the dirt to see the lofty summits to which God has called them. Life has no divine dimension.

The summer after I graduated from high school, I traveled with a companion to Yosemite Park for a few days. We arrived after nightfall. By the time we reached our camp ground, it was quite dark. We had no flashlights and groping along through the trees, came to what appeared to be a level spot. We threw down our bedrolls and crawled in. So far as we could see, Yosemite was no different than any other place in the mountains. The trees were dark against the starlight overhead. It appeared that we were alone. Weary from the day, we soon dropped into a deep slumber. It was rather late the next morning when we awakened. As consciousness returned, I looked up through the trees to a beautiful blue heaven. Towering majestically on either side were the sheer granite walls of the canyon cliffs. A new dimension, a new perspective, a new world was apparent to me with the coming of light. Standing at the foot of our bedrolls I saw several children, and looking beyond them I realized that we were surrounded by campers in the midst of their household activities. The children were looking at us wonderingly as if to say, "How are these young men going to climb out of their bedrolls and dress in such a public spot?"—a question that was concerning us too, believe me!

Life can be like that. We throw down the bedrolls of existence. We don't see beyond the moment. There is no clear perspective. But when the light of Christ dawns, we see ourselves in the majesty of God's great plan. And without that light and purpose, we are unsuited literally for living.

Christ made it clear that the whole of life's meaning is found in knowing God. "This is life eternal, that they might know thee the only true God, and Jesus Christ whom thou hast sent" (*John 17:3*). To know Him and to fellowship with Him is life's highest privilege. To become like Him and to dwell with Him forever is life's true destiny. St. Augustine's dictum is true to Christ's word, "O Lord, Thou hast made us for Thyself. Our hearts are restless until they find their rest in Thee."

The realm of nature is also transformed in this view of Christ. All that we behold of physical phenomena around us is simply the robe of God, His garment of glory displaying His perfection and manifesting His power. The flowers of the field, the birds of the air, the hairs of the head are numbered and man as an individual is held in His mind and heart. He gives Himself to us through His ordered world.

Rough experiences and bitter facts appear to contradict this view. One might say, "Well, this is very fine but what about evil and injustice? What about sorrow and suffering? How can Christ say that life is glorious when confronted by these ugly facts? Let us simply point out that Jesus Himself went through the worst that the world could throw at Him, demonstrating for all time by His victory over sin and death, the Father's power and love. God will take the trusting life through any experience and prove His goodness.

> Truth forever on the scaffold,
> Wrong forever on the throne;
> Yet that scaffold sways the future,
> And behind the dim unknown
> Standeth God within the shadows
> Keeping watch above His own.
>   —James Russell Lowell

Observe how Christ relates all things to the Father. He said, "My meat is to do the will of him that sent me . . ." (*John 4:34*). The will of the Father was His satisfaction. It was also His joy. "I delight to do Thy will, O God . . ." (*Psalm 40:8*). When He prayed, He said, "Father, which art in heaven." When He ministered He witnessed to the Father, ". . . he doeth the works" (*John 14:10*). When He faced the suffering of the crucifixion, He accepted it in quiet confidence. ". . . shall I not drink the cup which the Father has given me?" (*John 18:11, RSV*). His last words on the cross were, "Father, into thy hands I commend my spirit . . ." All life issues from the Father. All life is accepted in obedience and trust from the Father and thus all of life becomes sacred, meaningful, redemptive in the Father.

Let me encourage you to believe what Jesus says about you. You are a living soul and God has made you for Himself. Our Lord reminds us that the body is important. It is not to be abused or despised. Christ is concerned with physical need. He feeds the hungry. He heals the sick and clothes the naked. He cleanses the leper and causes the lame to walk. He makes the deaf to hear, the dumb to speak, the blind to see. Jesus calls His disciples apart from their busy ministry to rest awhile, because He understands better than most of us today that we must go apart and rest with God or we come apart in the busyness of life. We observe that our Lord is concerned not only for man's soul, but his total being. In this world of destitution, physical suffering, loneliness, with its millions of refugees and war-blasted communities, Christians must be aware that their call is to minister with the Master to the physical needs of men.

Important as the body is, however, it is not the essence of life. It is the abode of something infinitely more important, man's eternal soul. So precious is this that our Lord warns, "For what is a man profited, if he shall gain the whole world, and lose his own soul? or what shall a man give in exchange for his soul?" (*Mat. 16:26*). "And fear not them which kill the body, but are not able to kill the soul: but rather fear him which is able to destroy both soul and body . . ." (*Mat. 10:28*). The body one day, will be laid aside, but the soul continues. The body is the scaffold erected for a few brief years, that within there might be the edifice of man's spirit which abides. The scaffold will be taken down, but the spiritual nature of man continues.

The soul has eternal destiny. The repentant, reconciled life which has turned in faith to God enters the Father's heart and home forever. But the unrepentant and unbelieving know eternal separation from God. This is a frightening thought and yet it comes from the One who supremely has taught us that God is love. If we accept the truth of the one, we must be prepared to accept the truth of the other. To the one, the Master calls, "Well done, thou good and faithful servant . . . enter thou into the joy of thy lord" (*Mat. 25:21*). But to the other, there will come the word, ". . . depart from me, all ye workers of iniquity" (*Luke 13:27*), and ". . . There shall be weeping and gnashing of teeth" (*Mat. 25:30*). So, you see, life is preparatory. It is decisive. It is a training ground. This is the field of great eternal decisions. What concerns us most? Our physical or our spiritual life, the body or the soul, our comforts or our character, immediate satisfactions or eternal values?

Let us imagine a young woman returning home on the night of her engagement. She enters her room with lovely cheeks flushed and her eyes sparkling. Opening the box containing her ring, she lets the light gleam and sparkle on the diamond nestling in its pillow of velvet. She breathes a long sigh of satisfaction. Can we conceive that she would then toss the ring carelessly into the corner of a drawer, but slip the box beneath her pillow? Let us take care that we do not toss our souls into a corner and concentrate upon the passing pleasures and satisfactions of the body.

Our Lord goes still further. He says there is a present purpose for the Father's children. He teaches that goodness is possible and necessary for men. Contemporary literature would refute this. In today's novel, the good characters are set forth as bad and the bad characters as good. A French phrase is descriptive, "Homesickness for the mud." But Jesus always holds before us the possibility and the necessity of goodness. "Be ye therefore perfect, even as your Father which is in heaven is perfect" (*Mat. 5:48*). In every generation there have been those who have found power in Christ to lift their lives like the lotus, to bloom in purity to the glory of God.

Then He tells us that man may know peace and satisfaction in this world. Oliver Wendell Holmes likened the personality to a stagecoach crowded with passenger inheritances from our ancestors. These inherited characteristics may journey together in harmony, but more than likely, they will travel in disharmony and conflict. It is bad enough to have inherited conflicts within, but what chance do we have of an enjoyable ride when all kinds of troubles climb on board from without and begin to bounce us about?

It is not surprising that few hearts know peace and quiet contentment. Through all the turbulence of Jesus' journey with its opposition and outrage, denials and desertion, beatings and blasphemies, pain and death, He never lost His deep inner peace, save for that moment of dereliction when the Father's face was hidden as Christ bore our sins. He was united in a single, profound, pure purpose. There was about Him a remarkable single-mindedness. He was absolutely at home with Himself and with the Father. He reconciled and adjusted the conflicts which we feel so keenly and made them His servants. This divine peace is His legacy to us. "Peace I leave with you, my peace I give unto you: not as the world giveth, give I unto you. Let not your heart be troubled, neither let it be afraid" (*John 14:27*). "The peace of God, which passeth all understanding . . ." is the inheritance of those who, with Christ, make the Father's heart their home.

An old martyr was being burned at the stake and as the preparations were completed the martyr turned to his judge and said, "Sir, I would that you would come and place your hand over my heart and see whose heart beats the faster!" For you see, the true child of God who dwells deep in the Father can move through life's severest testing with a calm heart.

I have more to learn about myself from the Master. He tells me that I am a living soul. He also tells me that I am a lost soul until I return to the Father's heart and the Father's home. The worst thing in the world is not ignorance or misfortune. The worst thing in the world is not even death. The worst thing in the world is sin. Sin is anything and everything that separates us from God and from our brother. Jesus compresses the awful consequences of sin into one word, "lost." Into that single word of four letters, we can let our imagination pack all the doom and dereliction conceivable. We cannot exaggerate it. Sin loses us to love. Sin loses us to our true service. Sin loses us to God's fellowship. Sin loses us to God's destiny. The Christ of the gospels is not just a religious teacher handing out truths to be accepted or rejected according to men's fancy. But we find Him on a mission of terrible urgency, "For the Son of man is come to seek and to save that which was lost" (*Luke 19:10*). That mission consumes Him. Calvary is the true measure of what Jesus teaches about man's need. He is willing to lay down His life that the lost may be found, that man, separated by sin from his Father, may enter into the light and life of His presence. The note of "lostness" sounds through the Bible from start to finish.

But "lostness" is a minor note in the gospels. The major note is to be "found." It rings joyfully and triumphantly from every page. The woman loses her coin, but she will not rest until she finds it. One lost sheep is out in the wilderness, but the Shepherd will not rest until, forsaking the ninety and nine, He finds the lost sheep and carries it on His shoulders, rejoicing that the lost is found. The repentant prodigal turns his face homeward. The father seeing his son, yet a great way off, runs, embraces him and welcomes him back. God is like that, Jesus says.

To reach us where we are in our lostness, Christ Himself

has come. He wants every man to know that whatever his condition, rich or poor, high or low, good or bad, He is willing to pardon him and impart the power of a new life.

The poor paralytic is laid at Jesus' feet. Our Lord looks at this helpless, wasted wretch and moved with compassion, says, ". . . Son, be of good cheer, thy sins be forgiven thee" (*Mat. 9:2*). The Scribes and Pharisees murmur among themselves, ". . . Who can forgive sins, but God alone?" (*Luke 5:21*). Jesus knew their thoughts and asked, ". . . What reason ye in your hearts? Whether is easier, to say, Thy sins be forgiven thee; or to say, Rise up and walk?" (*Luke 5:22–23*). "But that ye may know that the Son of man hath power upon earth to forgive sins . . . I say unto thee, Arise, and take up thy couch, and go into thine house" (*Luke 5:24*). Immediately he is healed, and rising, he takes up his bed and walks, glorifying God. Wherever there is a moral or a spiritual cripple, helpless and unable to stand, there is a loving Father and a powerful Saviour able to make him whole.

Peter wanted to follow Christ and affirmed boldly before the disciples, "Though I should die with thee, yet will I not deny thee . . ." (*Mat. 26:35*). Yet he denied his Lord around the fire and moved out into the night to weep bitterly. Many of us have started confidently to do right in our own strength, only to find that we have failed miserably. We need the gift that Christ gave Peter. Jesus found him, forgave him, and breathed upon him the power of the Holy Spirit. He made him to stand as a rock and a pillar of the church of God. Christ wants us to know that we are loved, and that the love of God for us is a transforming love—a love that forgives, ennobles, and overcomes.

The thief upon the cross deserved to die because of his rebellion and crime. In his agony he called to Christ, the Man on the central cross, "Lord, remember me when thou comest into thy kingdom. And Jesus said unto him, Verily I say unto thee, To day shalt thou be with me in paradise" (*Luke 23:42–43*).

The meaning of the cross can be simply stated—though we are lost, we are loved of God. That love, so completely given in His Son, is seeking us. When we receive it and trust the Giver, we are found of Him and find ourselves. We have the answer to the biggest question life asks. "For God so loved the world, that he gave his only begotten Son, that whosoever believeth in him should not perish, but have everlasting life" (*John 3:16*).

WHAT JESUS SAYS ABOUT GOODNESS

*A good man out of the good treasure of his heart bringeth
forth that which is good; and an evil man out of the evil
treasure of his heart bringeth forth that which is evil: for
of the abundance of the heart his mouth speaketh.*

Luke 6:45

THE ETHICAL TEACHINGS OF JESUS CHRIST EVIDENCE HIS DIVINE
authority. We have already touched upon the uniqueness of
Christ's teaching about God and man. Now let us consider
what He has to say about goodness.

When the teachings of the great philosophers and religious
leaders of the ages are held up to the effulgent light which was
brought into the world by Jesus Christ, they pale like the
moon before the rising sun. Where may one find in non-Christian systems the moral concepts of Christ on the subjects of
righteousness, truth, purity, and love? None have been able
to match or excel the standard Jesus gives for life. He remains
the Master Teacher of human goodness.

Christ teaches us that goodness is from within, that it is a
matter of the heart. "A good man out of the treasure of his

heart bringeth forth that which is good; and an evil man out of the evil treasure of his heart bringeth forth that which is evil: for of the abundance of the heart his mouth speaketh" (*Luke 6:45*). From Mark's Gospel we learn, "There is nothing from without a man, that entering into him can defile him: but the things which come out of him, those are they that defile the man" (*Mark 7:15*).

In that day as in ours, goodness was considered to be largely a matter of obedience to certain laws, an outward conduct conforming to the accepted pattern. For example, the Pharisees meticulously obeyed all the laws and traditions of their fathers. They labored assiduously to keep every little rule. They fasted twice in the week. They tithed. But Jesus said they neglected mercy and truth, the weightier matters of the law, which are of the heart. Out of their narrow, religious activities they were endeavoring to weave some sort of garment of goodness to cover an unchanged heart. But real goodness lies within. Jesus stands before us and simply asks, "Show me your heart."

In a searching passage in the Sermon on the Mount, our Lord goes behind the letter of the law to demand obedience to its spirit. He adds a whole new dimension of moral and spiritual depth to the Commandments of the Old Testament. "Think not that I am come to destroy the law, or the prophets; I am not come to destroy, but to fulfill" (*Mat. 5:17*). He is saying, "I am come to fill out to the full the real intent of the law." He then proceeds to touch upon five Old Testament rules given to preserve the sanctity of life, and He transforms them by applying them to inner attitudes.

The first time a student peers through a microscope at a drop of tap water, he has an unforgettable experience. With his natural vision, it seems pure and uncontaminated, but through the microscope he is amazed to discover that one little drop of water contains a whole universe of life, and some of the creatures that come into view are rather frightening. I remember the time when I sat down with the Sermon on the Mount and let the Lord focus my attention upon the real meaning of the Commandments. A new world opened up with God's truth and goodness shining within, and some rather alarming things came into view as I looked at my life in the light of Jesus Christ.

Consider this commandment. Jesus continues, ". . . It was said by them of old time, Thou shalt not kill . . . But I say unto you that whosoever is angry with his brother without a cause shall be in danger of the judgment . . ." (*Mat. 5:21, 22*). Old Testament law condemned the act. Jesus condemns the attitude. The old law prohibited the deed, but Jesus prohibited the desire. The old forbade the murder, but Jesus forbade the anger out of which murder is born. One strikes at the fruit. The other goes back to the root. One apprehends the criminal when his hand has already struck the blow and is red with blood. The other apprehends him when hatred is born. What lies in our heart? Is there resentment, hostility, desire for retaliation, bitterness, lack of forgiveness and love there? Jesus warns that out of this spirit murder comes. They are qualitatively the same. They differ only in degree. So He asks, "Show me your heart." He penetrates within.

Another commandment is brought to our attention. ". . . It was said by them of old time, Thou shalt not commit adultery: but I say unto you, That whosover looketh on a woman to lust after her hath committed adultery with her already in his heart" (*Mat. 5:27, 28*). The sin of impurity is a blight and a curse upon society. It destroys true love and undermines the home. It defiles the soul; it disrupts and demoralizes the personality. Impurity, too, begins within. It consists not only in the act, but in the thought. Long before the science of psychology was born, our Lord taught the truth that ideas are motor and that "what a man thinketh in his heart, so is he." Let a life harbor lust, and soon lust will enslave the life. Purity is a matter of mind and of heart as well as of body.

Today, America knows a tidal wave of immorality. The dikes of moral restraint are breaking down, and a flood of impurity has been loosed across the land. What is happening among the boys in the Armed Forces overseas, thousands of miles away from home, is a shameful and degrading story of widespread impurity. Delinquency among our teen-agers is becoming a matter of public alarm. Behind many of our broken homes and embittered hearts today lies the sin of impurity.

The glory of the gospel is that it produces a new heart. It goes to the root of the need. Christ does not attempt to change the baser passions of the soul, to inhibit and suppress primitive impulses. Rather, He redirects these energies into new channels, imparting new desires, new affections, new love. He produces new men and women who enter into new relationships and respond in new ways. See what wonders He has wrought! In His hand, marriage is sanctified in spiritual oneness, and the family becomes the household of God, finding, in His forgiveness and love, a basis for mutual understanding and trust.

Christ has emancipated womanhood, elevating her to a position of dignity and honor. He has purified love, purging it from selfishness and lust. He has freed the human spirit that it might be pure and self-giving, fulfilling that which was in the Creator's mind when He gave us these desires. With eyes of penetrating purity, our Lord stands before us and simply asks, "Show me your heart."

Let us consider a new dimension to truth which we find here. Our Lord speaks of the matter of oaths. ". . . It hath been said by them of old time, Thou shalt not forswear thyself, but shalt perform unto the Lord thine oaths: But I say unto you, Swear not at all; neither by heaven; for it is God's throne . . . But let your communication be, Yea, yea; Nay, nay: for whatsoever is more than these cometh of evil" (*Mat.* 5:33, 34, 37). In other words, our Lord is saying that new character makes old sanctions unnecessary. If a man speaks the truth from his heart, he needs no other buttressing to support his words. As a matter of fact, there is no other way to insure truth or justice for men apart from a reverence for the law of God in the human heart. Unless there is an inner control of conduct and an inner respect for righteousness, neither social sanctions nor political systems can ever bring about justice. Lawlessness within, issues in chaos and tyranny without. Just survey the modern scene.

An authority on Latin America recently stated that that area of the world's greatest need is not for technical skills and advice, but for moral and spiritual character. Many of Latin America's problems stem from moral deficiencies and spiritual inadequacies. For example, wherever there are city traffic signals, there are always several armed policemen to enforce the law.

A Latin-American visitor to the United States was astonished when the bus on which he was riding stopped unbidden at a railroad crossing. The track was rusty and obviously unused. Yet the bus came to a stop; the driver looked both ways and went on across the track.

"Why did you stop the bus?" the visitor asked curiously. "Obviously there is no train coming." The driver answered, "It is the law." The visitor to our country was frankly amazed and impressed that the mere existence of a law could evoke obedience without a compulsive hand near by. But unless there is respect for law, ordered not by the fear of pressure from without, but by the desire of responsibility from within, there cannot be a just and free society, undergirded with citizens of true character.

What controls operate in your life? This is an honest question and it deserves an honest answer. Am I good because of the requirements of society, because I fear what others will think or say, because I do not wish to arouse the disfavor of others or incur the penalty of the law? Am I good because I am compelled to be good, or am I good because I really want to be good? Many people are outwardly good because they are afraid to do wrong, rather than because they are in love with the right. Jesus simply asks, "Show me your heart."

Christ further teaches us that goodness is grounded in two basic virtues, humility and love. This is the soil out of which all goodness grows, and, without this base, real virtue does not take root. Humility is the opposite of pride—that damnable thing that has cursed the race, vaunted itself above the authority of God and the rights of our fellow man. Pride is the stubborn core of sin. Jesus came into the world to break the power of pride, to put self back in subordination to God, where it belongs and where it finds its true freedom, peace, and joy. His own life is a demonstration of true humility and absolute trust in the Heavenly Father. "I am meek and lowly," Jesus says, yet His humility is attended with glorious strength and freedom.

There is a remarkable passage in the second chapter of Philippians which no one has really plumbed. "Let this mind be in you, which was also in Christ Jesus: who, being in the form of God, thought it not robbery to be equal with God: but made himself of no reputation, and took upon him the form of a servant, . . . and being found in fashion as a man, he humbled himself, and became obedient unto death, even the death of the cross" (*Phil. 2:5–8*). We see now the humility of our Lord, the very Son of Heaven, who came to be born in a lowly stable, toiled with His hands, moved among men as a servant, not doing His own pleasure or standing on His own rights, but humbling Himself, even to dying the death of the cross for sinful people. Seeing these manifestations, one can only utter,

> When I survey the wondrous cross
> On which the Prince of Glory died,
> My richest gain I count but loss,
> And pour contempt on all my pride.

If we are acquainted at all with Jesus, He has done something to our pride. If we know Him as our Lord, He has crippled its power. Now there is a desire to know His humility. Do not think for a moment that this humility is weakness, a retiring acquiescence to evil in the world. Not at all. Jesus said, "Blessed are the poor in spirit; for theirs is the kingdom of heaven. Blessed are the meek: for they shall inherit the earth." "The poor in spirit" are those who have nothing in themselves, and "the meek" are those who want nothing for themselves. Theirs is the Kingdom of Heaven. They inherit the earth. Everything is theirs. They move among men not to dominate them, but to get underneath and lift them. This is Christ's kind of life. "He came not to be ministered unto, but to minister and to give his life a ransom for many." Think what true humility would bring to us. Humility in the home would produce peace. In human relationships, it would foster understanding and harmony. Towards God, humility would lead to faith and fellowship. Towards our Lord Jesus Christ, it would bring salvation and joy. "Come unto me, all ye that labour and are heavy laden, and I will give you rest. Take my yoke upon you, and learn of me; for I am meek and lowly in heart: and ye shall find rest unto your souls" (*Mat. 11:28, 29*). He asks, "Show me your heart."

Humility is to be united to love. Love is the royal law of God. This is the first and great commandment. Christ taught that we are to love God with all our heart and our neighbor as ourself. Love is the new commandment, ". . . That ye love one another; as I have loved you . . ." (*John 13:34*). We are to love our enemies. This royal law of God takes precedence over every other law. If we fail here, we fail all along the line. No imposing array of virtues, no pious devotion, no long prayers or rigorous religious observances will please God unless there is love in the heart. This is the ultimate test of true religion and a true relationship with God and conformity to His Spirit. For it is written, "He that loveth not knoweth not God; for God is love" (*I John 4:8*). And when we place our small, selfish hearts alongside the great heart of God, we begin to understand how abysmal is our lovelessness, how immense our need.

How little we really care about the suffering or the sorrowing. What is our concern for those who are caught in the coils of sin or who grope in the darkness of despair? When Jesus saw the people as sheep having no shepherd, He had compassion on them. Above the city of Jerusalem, knowing something of its sorrow and suffering, of its awful sin and darkness, He cried aloud, "O Jerusalem, Jerusalem . . . how often would I have gathered thy children together, even as a hen gathereth her chickens under her wings, and ye would not!" (*Mat. 23: 37*). He wept over the city. But we seldom, if ever, shed a tear over our own community and its needs. With His friends by the tomb of Lazarus, Jesus wept, entering with sympathy into the grief of those about Him. Rarely do we weep with those who weep around us. Jesus cared. "Other sheep I have, which are not of this fold: them also I must bring. . . ." "The good shepherd giveth his life for the sheep." Yet all around us are wandering sheep, struggling to find their way into life. They are without Christ, without God, and without hope in the world. Do we really care? Not as He cares. We need His love deep in our hearts.

A Quaker woman accompanied by a young friend was walking down the street. She was approached by one in a tempest of anger who proceeded to administer a tongue lashing. But the Quaker woman took it graciously. She did not retaliate, although she was not to blame. After the episode had passed, her companion said wonderingly, "I marvel that you responded to her with such real Christian grace." "Ah," said the Quaker woman, "thee did not see the boiling within!" There was no boiling within our Lord. From the heart, He loved, purely, openly, naturally. He gave His compassion in an overflowing measure. Grudgingly we parcel out our love under compulsion. We need His love.

The nature of real love is revealed supremely by His death. He said, "Greater love hath no man than this, that a man lay down his life for his friends" (*John 15:13*). Then He showed us the infinite measure of His love. I see the disciples deserting Him and denying Him, leaving Him to suffer alone. Yet His love for them is stronger than their shame. Behold Him standing before His enemies, falsely accused, mocked, railed, tortured. I hear the crowd shout, "Crucify him! Away with him! We will not have this man to rule over us." I follow Him through the mocking multitude as He staggers under the burden of His cross. Now they drive great nails through hands that reached out only to love. With a sickening lurch, the cross is uplifted in its socket and Jesus hangs in agony. A monstrous, taunting jeer is hurled at Him by the multitude. "He saved others; himself he cannot save. . . ." They enjoy His anguish. For a moment His eyes are uplifted to heaven. His lips part in prayer. With labored breath, He pleads, "Father, forgive them, for they know not what they do."

No, He did not come down from the cross. He was held there not by the spikes of the soldiers, but by His own omnipotent love. He suffered to bring salvation to sinners, to open fainting hearts to the love of God. "God commendeth his love toward us, in that, while we were yet sinners, Christ died for us" (*Romans* 5:8). Writes the chief of sinners, "He loved me and gave himself for me." Thus for all men and for all time, our Lord has given to us the divine standard of goodness. Love is a mighty, self-giving passion, moving out even to those who do not want it. Jesus stands before us and says, "Show me your heart." With flushed cheeks and stricken soul, I dare not.

But there is another truth the Master teaches, without which His high and holy standard of goodness would lead us to despair. Goodness comes from God. We do not achieve goodness. It is a gift received from His hand. "We love him," writes the Apostle, "because he first loved us." Our love is kindled with the flame of His compassion. What made Peter good—Peter with his temper, impetuosity, failure, and denial? Was it resolution, moral endeavor? No! Jesus Christ made Peter good and Jesus Christ made Peter great. After the resurrection, Jesus found His fallen friend, forgave him and restored him and filled him with His Holy Spirit. When one has known forgiveness and the restoring grace of God in Jesus Christ, there is a mark upon his soul. In gratitude, he wants to be like the One who has redeemed him. "The love of Christ constraineth me," cries Paul, the Apostle.

In George Bernard Shaw's *Saint Joan,* Joan says, "If I go through fire, I shall go through it to their hearts forever and ever." Jesus, the Son of God in humility and love, went through the fire of the cross for us that He might move into our hearts forever. He makes us good by His great goodness.

A brilliant German said of Goethe, the poet, "Other men I love with my own strength, but he teaches me to love with his strength." That's it! It is only when Christ with His strength lives within that we are good.

I am painfully aware of my lack of natural goodness, my pride and lovelessness. I am keenly conscious that in the battle for goodness, time and again I am thrown back in miserable defeat. But I know that Jesus Christ comes to a man, and when He is trusted and obeyed, He gives His purity, His humility, His love. Our small hearts are made good because He imparts to them His love and goodness. He calls, "Give me your heart!"

WHAT JESUS SAYS ABOUT SUFFERING AND EVIL

And Jesus went forth, and saw a great multitude, and was moved with compassion toward them, and he healed their sick.

Matthew 14:14

HIGH ON THE LIST OF HUMAN CONCERNS ARE THOSE OF SUFFER-ing and sorrow. Suffering not only brings discomfort, but it also produces doubt. It not only presents pain, but it also presents a problem. Let us then turn to the Master Teacher with our difficulties and listen to what He has to say about the problem of suffering.

According to Jesus, suffering and sorrow are unnatural in the order of God. Pain is an intruder, an evil interloper who has invaded God's domain. Pain is a thief who has broken into the household of the Father to torment the children and steal their happiness from them. Jesus makes it very clear that suffering does not originate with the Father. God does not enjoy the agonies and the sorrows of His children. Our Lord responded to suffering with love and sympathy. We read, "But when he saw the multitudes, he was moved with compassion on them, because they fainted, and were scattered abroad, as sheep having no shepherd" (*Mat. 9:36*). The word "compassion" in the original language means "to suffer with—to be identified with the anguish and woe of another." Whenever our Lord saw need or sensed sorrow, He joined His heart to the afflicted. He always took the part of the sufferer against the suffering, the part of the sorrowing one against the grief, of the sick one against the illness, of the weak against his infirmity.

A leper cast out of society because of his contagious disease sees the Master passing by and cries out to Him, "Lord, if thou wilt, thou canst make me clean" (*Mat. 8:2*). "Lord, if you are willing, if you really want to, you can heal me." Our Lord moves toward him, and laying that loving hand upon the diseased flesh, He answers, "I am willing . . . (I really want to) . . . Be thou cleansed." And the leper was healed.

A blind beggar on the streets of Jericho learns that the Son of David is passing by. From the thronged roadside he calls, ". . . Jesus, thou Son of David, have mercy on me" (*Mark 10: 47*). Those around him endeavor to quiet him. They feel he may be disturbing important matters in the Master's ministry. But Jesus catches that plaintive cry above the confusion, and He asks that the blind man be brought to Him. Then, putting the sightless one in the very center of the circle, He says, "What wilt thou that I should do unto thee?" The man replies, ". . . Lord, that I might receive my sight" (*Mark 10:51*). Immediately, his eyes are opened.

Others may not be sensitive to the call of the suffering, but Jesus always is. There is not one instance in all the gospel record where anyone came to Jesus with an anxiety or an illness but that the Master ministered to him and healed him. His arms always reach out to human need.

The shortest verse in the Bible describes Jesus as He stands beside the tomb of Lazarus with the mourning sisters and friends. "Jesus wept" (*John 11:35*). There is a volume of truth in these two terse words. Look at them in the light of Christ's comment, ". . . he that hath seen me hath seen the Father . . ." (*John 14:9*). He is saying, if you want to know what God is like, observe Me. If you desire to understand how He feels and responds, look at Me. In the presence of sorrow, Jesus wept. Through Him, we learn that God is not a far-off, impersonal God of chance. He has not placed humanity on this speck of cosmic dust, and then, having wound up all the laws, He has not turned His back on us to let us sweat it out alone. He hears the cry of people. Christ reveals to us that God really cares. The measure of His concern is the length to which He has gone to redeem us from suffering and sorrow, even to His own anguish and death on the cross.

Jesus met suffering with more than sympathy. He strongly opposed it. In the mind of our Lord, suffering is joined to evil. The major source of most human misery is sin. The reign of God is one of peace and joy, of light and life, but man has chosen to revolt against his Maker. He has set himself up as God. In arrogance and pride, he has deified his own will and made it supreme, rather than coming humbly and trustfully to place his life in the hand of God. Mankind is like the Prodigal. We have gathered together what we thought was rightfully our own, gone into a far country, and wasted our substance. Now we find ourselves out with the hogs in great hunger of soul. Let us not blame the Father's heart nor the

Father's house. We have chosen our own way and brought on ourselves the major part of our suffering.

Charles Kingsley wrote, "Just as a wheel in a piece of machinery punishes itself when it is out of gear, so humanity punishes itself when it is withdrawn from the will of God." Think for a moment of all the agony and grief which our own selfishnesses have brought upon us. Consider what hate, envy, and lust have brought to the human race. The conflicts of society about us are largely the reflection of deep conflicts in the human spirit.

A friend of mine who is a serious student of philosophy told me, "My experiences in the last World War shook my faith. I felt it difficult to reconcile carnage and destruction with God, but now I see this in a new light. The twentieth century is the age of revolt against God and of an idolatrous worship of man. God has been ignored. His way has not been followed. His will has been rejected. Christ teaches us to live together as brethren in truth and goodness. We are finding out the hard way what happens to us when we choose a different path."

Robert Browning has said, "God's in His heaven; all's right with the world." But the fact is that God left His heaven to invade human history in the Person of Christ because there was so much wrong with the world. He came to challenge this intruder, this alien evil, and to cast it out. One day His will shall be done on earth as it is in heaven, and that will be the day of deliverance from sorrow and suffering. "God shall wipe away all tears from their eyes; and there shall be no more death, neither sorrow, nor crying, neither shall there be any more pain . . ." (*Rev. 21:4*).

Now if Christ has come to put an erring world right, then you and I must take our stand with Him and enlist our energies to march against evil wherever it is found. If "God so loved the world that he gave his only begotten Son . . ." and if Christ cared enough to suffer for the suffering, then we too must be sensitive to human need and keep our ears open to every cry.

"Well," one may reply, "suffering is understandable in some cases but not in every case. How do you explain the suffering of the godly and the innocent?" When the wicked suffer, we sense that there is a factor of justice involved, but what happens when the righteous suffer? We read that Herod, the wicked king, was eaten of worms. Certainly, I can understand that. He gets what is coming to him. He sowed the wind; he reaps the whirlwind. Hitler died in a flaming chancellery. That makes sense. But Jesus! Jesus was crucified between two thieves. What do we do with that?

Let us go a step farther with the Master Teacher and His teaching about pain and evil. Though unnatural, suffering, Jesus teaches, is inevitable in this kind of world. Even the sinless Son of God suffered. The looming specter of the crucifixion distressed the disciples. Christ did not hide from them what was going to happen. "Remember the word that I said unto you, The servant is not greater than his lord. If they have persecuted me, they will also persecute you . . ." (*John 15:20*). Do not be surprised if you are thrust into the prison-house of pain. Look how they are treating Me. But do not despair; there is a way through. ". . . In the world, ye shall have tribulation; but be of good cheer; I have overcome the world" (*John 16:33*). The mystery of evil in a world ruled by God is not so baffling as the mystery of goodness in a godless world. It is a goodness that is basic and wonderful. It is a goodness that exists to a far greater degree than we realize.

One of the tragic fallacies current today is the proposition that the good should not suffer, and that if one is experiencing sickness or sorrow, it is because he does not have the right faith or lead the right kind of life. Adversity is due to some kind of moral or spiritual inadequacy. Peace of mind and prosperity cults abound, saying, "Come join us. Practice our formula and you will find all your problems solved, all your difficulties dissolved, all distresses driven away." But that is not what we read in the New Testament. God does deliver His people from trouble, but not always. Simon Peter, a pillar of the church, was thrust into prison, scourged, and finally, according to tradition, was crucified upside down. His faithfulness did not procure a pass from persecution and pain. James, the brother of John, one of the closest companions of Christ, was imprisoned and beheaded by a wicked king. Paul, the Apostle, whose life of intense devotion has burned like a pure flame of light through the centuries, wrote: "From henceforth let no man trouble me: for I bear in my body the marks of the Lord Jesus" (*Gal. 6:17*). To be a follower of Jesus, for the first century church, meant suffering. It was the badge of their devotion. "Yea, and all that will live godly in Christ Jesus shall suffer persecution" (*II Tim. 3:12*).

Supremely, Jesus teaches that suffering is not only unnatural in God's order and inescapable in the world today, but that it is also usable for the child of God. Among the many unique aspects of Jesus' ministry is His revolutionary approach to suffering. He declares that every experience which comes to us, within the permissive will of God, may be made to minister to us and used as a means of bringing glory to God. Whatever comes to us in this life may be our servant and an instrument of blessing.

There are three basic attitudes towards suffering. One may resent it, lash out violently against it, blame others, blame circumstances, blame God, and let it poison the soul with bitterness. That attitude is deadly. It corrodes the heart like acid. It sickens the spirit. It even affects the body. Never treat difficulty that way. It simply turns the cutting edge of trouble back upon oneself.

Another attitude toward suffering is to be stoical about it, to say, "Since I cannot extricate myself from this situation, I will take it without whimpering." One marshals his resources, gathers together his willpower, firms the upper lip, and thrusts out the chin, saying, "All right. I can take it." Now of course, that is better than resentment, but it isn't enough. Stoicism is brittle, and if the pressure is strong enough, it will break, and the inner defenses will be shattered.

Our Lord teaches us neither to resent suffering nor simply to endure it, but rather to accept it with gratitude. He encourages us to reach out with both hands and embrace with thanksgiving whatever comes to us as obedient and trusting children of God. The supreme demonstration of this attitude is found in Christ's own crucifixion. Here is evil and anguish at its zenith, the problem stripped naked and thrown out into the light for all to see—Jesus, the holy, loving Son of God crucified. Observe His spirit of submission to the Father's will. ". . . Father, if it be possible, let this cup pass from me: nevertheless not as I will, but as thou wilt" (*Mat. 26:39*). In Gethsemane's garden, praying until sweat as great drops of blood fell to the ground, He entered into full understanding of the Father's will. He arose to embrace the cross with assurance. Henceforth, the crucifixion was His servant, an instrument to be used for man's good and God's glory. ". . . the cup which my Father hath given me, shall I not drink of it?" (*John 18:11*).

Pilate said to Him, ". . . knowest thou not that I have power to crucify thee, and have power to release thee?" (*John 19: 10*). And our Lord replied, "Thou couldst have no power at all against me, except it were given thee from above . . ." (*John 19:11*). His poise and peace remained unshaken.

Then came Calvary. In the eyes of the ancient world, crucifixion was such a loathesome torture, disgrace, and death that it was not mentioned in respectable company. Jesus suffered its agony physically. Emotionally He suffered its burning shame and mockery. Spiritually He suffered separation from the Father. He bore our sin vicariously. There was suffering in His cry that we can never know, "My God, my God, why hast thou forsaken me?"

Yet Jesus accepted the cross with thanksgiving and used it to conquer sin, suffering, and death for us. ". . . who for the joy that was set before him endured the cross, despising the shame, and is set down at the right hand of the throne of God" (*Heb. 12:2*). Watching Jesus, we learn that we can take the worst things, and by God's transforming power, they can become our servants, pulpits from which to proclaim the glory of our Lord.

James has a significant sentence in the beginning of his epistle. J. B. Phillips has translated it, "When all kinds of trials and temptations crowd into your lives, my brothers, don't resent them as intruders, but welcome them as friends" (*James 1:2*). Did I not say that this attitude was revolutionary? How do you welcome difficulties? When sorrow comes stalking into your heart, what do you do with it? When sickness lays you on your back, how do you handle it? When your

heart is breaking because of some distressing personal relationship, where do you go with your trouble?

It is not that the Christian is deferred from these experiences or is immune to them, but the Christian can do something creative with his suffering. Suffering can become his
servant. This we can verify if we truly trust Jesus Christ. He
will use trouble for our good. "All things are for your sakes . . ."
writes the Apostle (*II Cor. 4:15*).

The early Christians took suffering as an opportunity. When
they were beaten, they went on their way, rejoicing that they
were counted worthy to suffer shame for the name of Christ.
In prison, they sang praises to God. In death, they prayed for
their tormentors and saw heaven's glory. Let us call Peter
before us. "Peter, you know what it is to grieve. There was
that dark night when you went out and wept bitterly over
your failure. What did you learn then?" And Peter replies,
"Beloved, think it not strange concerning the fiery trial which
is to try you, as though some strange thing happened unto
you: But rejoice, inasmuch as ye are partakers of Christ's suf-
ferings; that, when his glory shall be revealed, ye may be glad
also with exceeding joy" (*I Peter 4:12, 13*). ". . . though now
for a season, if need be, ye are in heaviness through manifold
temptations: that the trial of your faith being much more precious than of gold that perisheth, though it be tried with fire,
might be found unto praise and honour and glory at the ap-
pearing of Jesus Christ" (*I Peter 1:6, 7*). Peter would say, "In
the upper room when I boasted that I would be faithful unto
death to Christ, how little I knew of myself and my weakness.
I needed to be uprooted from vain self-confidence and planted
in God. During that dark night of despair, I found that even
the shame of my cowardice and denial could be used to bring

me to an end of myself and open new life through the risen Saviour. My confidence now, is not in myself but in Him."

Let us ask the Apostle Paul, "What about that thorn in the flesh, Paul, that stake upon which you are impaled?" "For this thing," he writes, "I besought the Lord thrice, that it might depart from me. And he said unto me, my grace is sufficient for thee. . . . Most gladly therefore will I rather glory in my infirmities, that the power of Christ may rest upon me . . . for when I am weak, then am I strong" (*II Cor. 12:8–10*). "And not only so, but we glory in tribulations also: knowing that tribulation worketh patience; And patience, experience; and experience, hope: And hope maketh not ashamed; because the love of God is shed abroad in our hearts by the Holy Ghost which is given unto us" (*Romans 5:3–5*). In effect, he is saying, "Whether my lot be adversity or prosperity, if I embrace it with trust and gratitude in God, it will serve my good and His glory."

God's main purpose is to make us like His Son. ". . . all things work together for good to them that love God, to them who are the called according to his purpose" (*Romans 8:28*). Everything is not good, but He will work for good in everything with those who love Him and are called to His purpose. His purpose is that we should be ". . . conformed to the image of his Son . . ." (*Rom. 8:29*). If, at times, He hammers the hard material of the heart with the mallet and chisel of distress and difficulty that we might be shaped into the likeness of our Lord Jesus Christ, let us be grateful. The twenty-third Psalm teaches us this truth also. "The Lord is my Shepherd; I shall not want. He maketh me to lie down in green pastures. . . ." The verb here is strong—He *compels* me, he *forces* me to lie down in green pastures.

An American traveling in Syria became acquainted with a shepherd. Each morning, he noticed the shepherd carrying food to the sheep. The traveler followed him one morning and found that he was taking the food to one sheep that had a broken leg. As he looked at the animal, he said to the shepherd. "How did the sheep break its leg? Did it meet with an accident—fall into a hole, or did some animal break the leg?" "No," said the shepherd, "I broke this sheep's leg myself." "You broke it yourself?" queried the surprised traveler. "Yes, you see this is a wayward sheep, it would not stay with the flock, but would lead the other sheep astray. Then it would not let me get near it. I could not approach it, and so I had to break the sheep's leg that it might allow me, day by day, to feed it. In doing this, it will get to know me as its shepherd, trust me as its guide, and keep with the flock."

"He maketh me to lie down. . . ." In our busyness, our absorption with life's pleasures and meaningless minutia, we do not heed the shepherd. We are too busy to pray, too busy to listen to God's word, too busy to know Him, to love Him and walk closely with Him. He makes us to "lie down in green pastures."

It is not the godly who complain of suffering if they understand God. Suffering is not a problem to the devout heart who has insight into God's ways. Perhaps to the unbeliever outside of Christ pain seems insoluble, but the trustful heart learns in every situation that God will meet him there. Christ, the good Shepherd, will transform trouble and bring light into darkness.

Catherine Marshall, widow of the late Peter Marshall, in a most remarkable way has let Christ transform suffering and sorrow for her. In her best-seller, *A Man Called Peter,* she tells of coming to Washington, D.C. She was busy with activities and responsibilities as the wife of one of the nation's leading pastors who had a ministry not only to the Senate as its Chaplain, but to the whole country. One day, Catherine Marshall faced her physician across his desk and heard his verdict of an examination. X-rays showed that she had tuberculosis and must have a period of complete rest. Her little world crashed around her. Oh, it was so important, she thought, that she be well! It was important to her husband, important to her little boy, important to the things of God. And in her heart, on the return journey, there was turmoil, fear, feverish anxiety.

As the weeks went by, she prayed urgently, seeking that God would do her will. "Heal me, Lord," was her burden. One day her husband left a little tract on the subject of healing on her bedside table. She read of a missionary who had been stricken in the midst of a flourishing work for Christ and for eight years lay on her back. All these long weary years, this one had prayed, "Lord, heal me in order that I might do your work. It seems to me, Lord, as though I deserve to be healed." And then, at long last, she submitted to the Lord, surrendering her way to Him. She said, "Thy will be done. What Thou dost desire for me, I want." And in that reconciliation, God touched her, blessed her, healed her.

Catherine Marshall read this story, and she saw her own life—shallow, dependent on others for spiritual strength, selfish and void of trust. She had wanted God to heal her in her way, in her time, as though she deserved it. "And now," she said, "with tears eloquent of the reality of what I was doing, I lay in bed and prayed, 'Lord I have done everything I've known how to do and it has not been good enough. I am desperately weary of the struggle of trying to persuade You to give me what I want. I am beaten, whipped, through. If You want me to be an invalid for the rest of my life, all right. Here I am. Do anything You like with me and my life.'" In that great commitment of submission and trust, Christ met her and transformed her life. He has given her a ministry which has inspired a nation. Through her testimony, thousands have seen new light in the dark valleys. So, my friend, when you submit to Christ, He meets you Himself and, in His wise and perfect way, transforms suffering, sweetens sorrow, and illumines life with the light of His Presence.

WHAT JESUS SAYS ABOUT THE GREATEST THING ON EARTH

Then said Jesus, Father, forgive them; for they know not what they do....

Luke 23:34

THE GREATEST THING ONE MAY KNOW IN THIS LIFE IS TO BE ASsured that he is right with God. As Jesus looked about Him, He saw tragic evidence of the terrible enemy of man. Wherever He went, He encountered those who were potential sons of God, but whose fellowship with the Father had been destroyed by this one enemy. Wherever He turned He observed the progress of humanity arrested by this one deadly foe—sin.

John Bunyan in *The Holy War* describes how Mansoul, the human heart, had opened the gate to Diabolus. Subjugating the inhabitants of the city, Diabolus led them in revolt against the King of Heaven and plunged the domain into darkness. The Prince Emmanuel came to recapture Mansoul for the Kingdom of God and set the captives free. This is the main mission of Jesus Christ.

Is it not strange that this generation which has suffered

so much from evil should be so indifferent or so ignorant of the reality of sin and its consequences? Chad Walsh has written, "We are suffering from mass rationalization." We know that humanity is in a mess, but we blame everything and everybody but ourselves. We will not face the obvious facts that war, oppression, crime, and most forms of human anguish have their source in the human heart. Is it not true that that which we see written large in the world around us is first to be read in our own hearts?

The Master Teacher points out that man's biggest problem is himself. He is "off center." Man is made to revolve around the holy will of the Father, to be centered in God, but man has chosen to be self-centered and self-willed. Like a derelict planet breaking from its orbit, he has plunged into spiritual darkness far from the light and life of God. To bring man back to the Father and restore the ruptured relationship, Christ the Saviour came.

Let us glance briefly at what the Master taught about sin —Public Enemy Number One. To Jesus, sin was anything and everything that separated man from his God and man from his neighbor. He taught that the fundamental barrier between man and God and man and his brother is not intellectual, but moral, not philosophical, but personal. "This is the condemnation, that light is come into the world, and men loved darkness rather than light, because their deeds were evil" (*John 3:19*). Or to put it in a positive way, He said, "If any man will do his will, he shall know of the doctrine, whether it be of God, or whether I speak of myself" (*John 7:17*).

God is not to be known by the massing of all the facts and phenomena of science. Nor is He to be discovered by some clever deductions of logic. If this were the basis for knowing God, only those with high I.Q.'s would be in the front rank spiritually; heaven would be made up of a group of carefully screened Ph.D.'s. The value of learning and the gifts of intelligence are not to be minimized, but the approach to God is a personal and moral one. What we do with the light we already have is all important.

Mansoul, duped by Diabolus, does not really want a king. That's the trouble. He wants to be king himself. He desires to make his own laws, order his own ways. This brings him into conflict with the real King. Sin is the willful transgression of the King's statutes, whether the commandments be written on tables of stone or impressed deep upon the conscience of the human heart. Royal edicts are posted in the consciences of every man. Their rejection brings ruin.

Jesus saw sin as a blow at a loving heart. Sin not only harms the sinner; it hurts the great loving heart of God. The deepest shadow in the parable of the Prodigal Son is not the suffering of the wayward boy, but the sorrow of a grieving and lonely father. To have a loved son who will not abide in the father's house, who does not choose the father's love, who does not want the father's will, but goes into a far country where he can live as he pleases, is by far the greater sorrow. This is the tragedy concerning man in the teaching of our Lord.

A few months ago my telephone rang early in the morning and I heard the voice of a man in a distant city. He told me that his son had run away from home and that he was being held in Juvenile Hall in the city in which I lived. He asked if I would stand by his son until he arrived to take him home. He told me of the background of the situation. There had been increasing friction between parents and son, defiance and disobedience on the part of the lad. He had drifted further and further into evil associations and companionships. Finally, there came the crisis. The boy had slammed the door in the face of his father and had chosen to go his own way. As I heard this story, I knew that the greater grief was not in the heart of the boy, but in the heart of the father. Sin is a grief to God.

Our Lord also took a serious view of sin. He hated passionately the evil things that shattered lives and separated men from God. In Milton's *Paradise Lost,* Satan has about him a certain glamour. He is "quite a boy," even in his evil ways. But there is no such attitude toward sin on the part of our Lord. He sees it as unmitigated and absolute wrong. The cross is the final measure of the seriousness of sin. Sin will crucify the Son of God, put to death everything that is good and decent and high and holy, and plunge the soul into darkness. Sin is terrible. Though it is not a cheerful subject, it may be good for us to see the consequences of evil through the eyes of Christ. Sin produces a tormented conscience. Although the prodigal son is held in the embrace of his father, his heart and his conscience are still in a far country, unreconciled and without peace.

No sooner had Peter denied his Lord and the Master had turned to look upon him, than he went out into the night and wept bitterly. There was no scourge upon Peter's back. There were no chains upon his wrists. Why then was he pulled into the darkness? He was driven by his sense of shame. So Judas Iscariot, after he had betrayed his Lord and heard the shouts of the crowd calling for the blood of Christ, found the thirty pieces of silver red-hot in his hand. Returning to the high priest and cohorts, he cried, "I have sinned in that I have betrayed innocent blood." They answered, "What is that to us? See thou to it!" With a cry of anguish, Judas flung the coins upon the pavement of the temple and rushed out into the night to take his life. Remorse lashed the soul of Judas.

Today, psychiatrists and therapists are besieged by patients whose sins will not let them sleep, whose sense of moral guilt and failure pursues them without pity, giving them no rest or inner peace. Perhaps you know the wretchedness of one before whom conscience stands with an accusing finger. What release and relief for such a one to know the pardon and peace of God which Jesus Christ brings to those who come in repentance to Him.

Another teaching of our Lord is that wrong doing results in an enslaved will. ". . . Whosoever committeth sin is the servant of sin" (*John 8:34*). There is no slavery as cruel, as intolerable as the slavery of sin. Let the alcoholic speak. Let the one in bondage to lust say a word. Let someone testify who knows the domination of a critical heart and a cutting tongue. Oh, the galling yoke of resentment, bitterness, and hate!

Jesus came "to preach deliverance to the captives . . . to set at liberty them that are bruised." He said, "If the Son therefore, shall make you free, ye shall be free indeed." Is there a higher liberty than this, to be free from ourselves, to live in the will of God? He teaches that the ultimate consequence of sin is judgment. How readily we accept the revelation of our Lord concerning God's love and mercy, but how slow we are to accept the revelation of His righteousness and justice! One fact shines out clearly in the teaching of our Lord. Sin, if persisted in, has consequences which reach beyond this life into eternity, and ultimately everyone will stand before the eternal justice of God. Consider the solemnity of the words which Jesus uses—"lost," "outer darkness," "everlasting fire," "weeping," "gnashing of teeth," "Depart from me, ye that work iniquity." Such terms convey a message of inexorable judgment.

"But," you say, "I don't believe in judgment. God it too good to damn a person, too good ever to punish." Whether we recognize it or not, we already live in a moral universe. Let a man trifle with truth, live a life of deceit, and he will see what it does to human relationships. Let a man abandon purity, embrace lust, and he will find out what it does to love. Let someone assert himself, trample upon the rights of others, and see what it does to friendships and family. Live solely for self and see the prison-house of selfishness which incarcerates the soul. Judgment is already operating.

It might be well to walk through the ruins of Berlin, sit down in the rubble, and meditate upon what history has to say about those who depart from the ways of God. Stand in front of some of the defaced monuments to Mussolini in North Africa and consider that the way of the transgressor is hard. What Christ is saying is that the law which is now in operation in human life extends into eternity. How great then, how incalculably great, is the gift of pardon! Our sins can be forgiven, the past covered, and the soul made right with a holy God. This is what Christ can do.

Most serious of all, sin separates us from the Father. Fellowship with the Father is the end and purpose of life. Sin carried the Prodigal away from the father's house, and beyond sight of the father's face. The father did not close the door.

The father did not bar the gate. He did not withdraw his favor. The Prodigal himself walked away into the far country.

Jesus seems particularly aware of the loneliness of the sinner. The prodigal finds himself in a far country beyond the fellowship of his friends, beyond the companionship of his brethren, beyond his father's face. The one lost sheep is alone in the wilderness. Can any greater goodness come to man than to be welcomed home to God? Is there any deeper satisfaction than the knowledge that one is found by his father and received into his heart forever? This is the satisfaction the Good Shepherd can bring to us.

A young couple were having difficulty with their small boy. As they sat down at the dinner table, they admonished, "Now, Johnny, if you misbehave again, you will have to eat alone in the kitchen." Johnny continued as though he had not heard. Time came for action, and so they took Johnny to the kitchen, put his plate upon the sideboard, and settled him on a stool. Firmly they said, "Johnny, you must eat alone, but we will remain until you have returned thanks." Johnny bowed his head and prayed, "I thank Thee, Lord, for preparing a table before me in the presence of mine enemies." But God does not take us apart, shut the door, and isolate us from Himself. In the Garden of Eden, it was God who called, "Adam, where art thou?" God was seeking. Adam was fleeing. It is sin that separates us from God. It is the Saviour who brings us back.

If the Master teaches the seriousness of sin, He also reveals the certainty of salvation. He is the sinner's Friend. We cannot miss this fact as we read the gospels. He sought sinners out. The self-righteous were scandalized. They said, "He receiveth sinners and eateth with them." But Jesus was seeking them that He might save them. He delighted to walk by the seashore, where the wrecks came in. He loved to take the battered driftwood of life in His strong hands and make it new for God. To the shameful woman of Samaria, rejected by those of her little village, He offered the cleansing water of life. To the quisling tax-collector, Zaccheus—up a tree and out on a limb—He called, "Make haste, and come down, for today I must abide at thy house." Christ transformed him, made him new. He stooped and washed the feet of Judas Iscariot in a last appeal of love. He prayed on the cross, "Father, forgive them, for they know not what they do," while a sea of hatred and cruelty rolled over Him. Jesus seeks the sinner. There is not one instance in all the gospels in which He rebukes the earnest, repentant heart, not one occasion in which He refuses to meet the need of the humble seeker. He ministers to all. He goes to the greatest lengths to reach all—even to the cross.

The record becomes exciting when we understand that Christ gives full and final forgiveness to the one penitent in heart. He restores him to fellowship with God without qualification, without probation, without insisting on certain requirements or regulations to be fulfilled. He immediately reconciles the sinner to God. A helpless paralytic is laid at His feet. The Saviour sees a deeper malady—a disease of the soul. "Son, be of good cheer, thy sins be forgiven thee. Arise, take up thy bed and go unto thy house." With cleansed heart and in newness of life, the man leaps up and goes his way praising God. The greater miracle is the healing of the soul.

A woman of notorious reputation enters the house of Simon the Pharisee, where Jesus is dining. Bathing His feet with her tears, she pours upon Him her devotion. Simon, knowing what kind of a woman she is, says to himself, ". . . This man, if he were a prophet, would have known who and what manner of woman this is that toucheth him: for she is a sinner" (*Luke 7:39*). Our Lord, knowing what was in the mind of Simon, said, ". . . Her sins, which are many, are forgiven: for she loved much . . ." (*Luke 7:47*). And turning to the woman, He adds, "Thy faith hath saved thee; go in peace" (*Luke 7:50*). Her tears were the tears of gratitude, of a heart already cleansed, of a life already at peace with the Father. Jesus gives immediate, full, and final forgiveness.

The thief upon the cross cries out, "Lord, remember me when thou comest into thy kingdom. . . ." And Jesus turns without hesitation and says, "To day, shalt thou be with me in paradise." Jesus gives immediate and complete restoration to God.

Shortly after the worst of the blitz, a visitor to London was walking down Old Bailey Street and saw the Statue of Justice towering above the ruin and rubble around it. It spoke to him of the truth that when man ignores the justice of God, chaos comes. As he was meditating, he saw, beyond the Statue of Justice, St. Paul's Cathedral. Across the dome, still intact, bright in the morning sunlight, shone a cross. Above the ruin of sin, there is the redemption of God. Christ came not only to point the way, but to be the Way, to reach down by His atoning death to lift us in mercy to God. There is salvation for the sinner. "For God so loved the world, that he gave his only begotten Son that whosoever believeth in him should not perish, but have everlasting life" (*John 3:16*). ". . . God was in Christ, reconciling the world unto himself, not imputing their trespasses unto them . . ." (*II Cor. 5:19*).

Dr. E. Stanley Jones tells of a boys' school in the old days of strict discipline. There was a rule that anyone caught stealing would be flogged in front of the class. A little hunchback was caught stealing a fellow student's lunch. He was called before the teacher, who said to the lad, "Take off your shirt for the beating." The boy, ashamed of his twisted spine, cried out "No! not that!" The large boy whose lunch he had stolen raised his hand and said, "Is there any reason why I may not take the beating for him?" The teacher thought for a moment. "No, not as far as I know." "Then sir, permit me." He went forward and took off his own shirt, receiving the lashing for the other boy.

This is the cross. God does not stand afar off as a judge without feeling. In the Person of Christ, the holy and righteous One reaches out to the world in compassion, carrying the full penalty and hurt of our sins. In justice, He forgives all who come in Christ's name to receive His pardon. Let me face myself, acknowledge my condition, give myself to God, and receive from Jesus Christ the greatest thing there is—forgiveness and a life in full fellowship with the Father.

WHAT JESUS SAYS ABOUT PRAYER

*And I say unto you, Ask, and it shall be given unto you;
seek and ye shall find; knock, and it shall be opened unto
you.*

Luke 11:9

JESUS PRAYED. THE CHRISTIAN NEEDS NO OTHER CALL TO PRAYER
than this. Because Jesus prayed, the necessity and validity of
prayer is established for all time. Because Jesus prayed, prayer
in the life of the believer should have priority and authority.
If the strong Son of God prayed, He who always walked in
fullness of fellowship with the Father, who never knew the
shadow of sin nor the blight of failure, whose personality
flashed with divine glory and whose mighty works demonstrated divine power, how much more do you and I, weak and
sinful mortals, need to seek the face of our Heavenly Father
in prayer.

The disciples sensed that prayer was the source of Jesus'
power and love. They said, "Lord, teach us to pray." For them,
prayer was complicated and difficult. It was regulated by
artificial rules and formulas. But Jesus prayed in simplicity,

reality, and power. He lifted His face to heaven and said "Father," and all of life was blessed in His prayer.

Let us join the disciples and sit at the feet of the Master Teacher in the school of prayer. Our textbook will be the Gospel of Luke because there are more illustrations, examples, and precepts on prayer in Luke's Gospel than in any other Book of the New Testament. It may well be called the gospel of prayer. It begins in prayer, it ends in prayer, and the central passage of the Book in the eleventh chapter concerns prayer. With the Book open before us, with our minds open to God and in dependence on the Holy Spirit, let us ask some simple questions about prayer.

Where shall we pray? When shall we pray? What shall we pray? Why should we pray?

By word and example, Jesus teaches us *where* to pray.

We are to pray in solitude. Christ is our pattern here. In Luke 5:16, we find that ". . . he withdrew himself into the wilderness, and prayed." In Luke 6:12, we read, ". . . he went out into a mountain to pray." In Luke 9:18, ". . . it came to pass as he was alone praying." Again and again in the gospel record we find Jesus withdrawing from the pressing throng around Him, going to a desert place, a wilderness or a mountain, to be alone in fellowship with His Father in heaven. He was always aware of the Father's presence, always sensitive to the Father's voice. He walked in uninterrupted communion with God. Yet He needed to be alone. As the organism needs oxygen for life, Jesus seemed to need these times when He could breathe deeply and purely of fellowship with the Father without interruption or distraction.

If prayer was necessary in the life of our Lord, how much more is it necessary for us. God pity us in this confused, cramped, and crowded day, when we are pushed into the thronging cities, blasted by radios and television, rushed by automobiles, and badgered by activities. We have nearly every kind of experience imaginable but being alone. We do not even know how to behave in solitude. It frightens us to be alone. Yet the Lord tells us, "Be still and know that I am God. . . ." For no one can really know God, hear the still, small voice of the Spirit, or enter into intimacy with the living Christ without being alone with God. Our Lord said in the Sermon on the Mount, "But thou, when thou prayest, enter into thy closet, and when thou hast shut thy door, pray to thy Father which is in secret; and thy Father which seeth in secret shall reward thee openly" (*Mat. 6:6*).

If we are to become acquainted in a real way with another person, we need to be alone with him. When the suitor meets the young woman of his choice and arranges to have a date with her on a certain evening, what does he do? Does he rush home to his family, particularly to little brother, and say, "Look, I have a date tonight with my girl friend. Come, get in the car and join us!" No! He wants to be alone because it is only as we are alone with another that we can learn to know that one.

We need to be alone with God.

> *Lord, I have shut the door,*
> *Whisper Thy will,*
> *While I have drawn apart*
> *While all is still.*

> —Wm. R. Runyan

If we do not have some time alone with God, it is no wonder that we fail to see His face through the day, nor that we are not sensitive to the touch of His hand as we walk the crowded paths of life.

Christ also teaches us to pray with others. Real fellowship in prayer has its rise alone with God, but it soon joins with other streams of prayer in "togetherness." Luke 9:8 records that Jesus took Peter, James, and John and went up into the mountain to pray. He joined His heart with others in prayer. "For where two or three are gathered together in my name, there am I in the midst of them" (*Mat. 18:20*). ". . . if two of you shall agree on earth as touching any thing that they shall ask, it shall be done for them of my Father which is in heaven" (*Mat. 18:19*). "If two of you shall agree"—the root of the word "agree" is the same as that from which we get the word "symphony." Prayer is like a symphony orchestra under the baton of the divine Maestro. Together, we may have an orchestration and harmony which is impossible alone. This harmony operates in two directions, with our brethren and with God.

To be sure, the musician must play his instrument alone. Alone he gains proficiency in its use and becomes familiar with the score. But he cannot have a full ministry of music until he has joined his instrument with others. We may find that our prayer life is like a thin, squeaking piccolo, but placed alongside the deep tones of a mature intercessor, the little prayer finds its place. Also, we learn to pray in fellowship with others. Prayer is more caught than taught. So if you are only praying by yourself, place your instrument of intercession beside others. You will find it filling out the inadequacy in your life.

Even as a strong rope is composed of small strands, prayers put together have strength. There is power in united prayer. Suppose that if as we worship in unity of mind and heart, we were to pray for one another, "Lord, teach us to pray. Make us aware that Thou art real and art ready to receive our intercession. Show us Jesus Christ as He really is. Meet us now." That kind of "togetherness" in prayer would produce a spiritual charge like that of a magnetic field around a magnet. The presence of God would be electric in the congregation. Suppose that together, we were to join in upholding our President before the Lord, praying for him in his responsibilities that his mind might be led in the light of truth, that his heart might be made courageous to do the right, and that his spirit might enter into full fellowship with his God. That kind of united prayer would have an impact which our isolated and separate intercessions could not produce. Or, if together each one of us in unity of purpose and faith, were to lift the torn and disunited lands of Asia, praying for justice and peace, there would be power. "Pray together," Jesus said. Praying needs focus, the direction of God's Word faced in a group, the fellowship of kindred minds, the power of corporate courage and convictions.

Then I learn from Jesus Christ that I may pray anywhere and everywhere. He prayed in the mountain and He prayed in the field. He prayed under the olive-trees and in the temple. He prayed as He walked along the roads of Galilee. He prayed on the cross. I may pray anywhere. Dr. Frank Laubach in his book, *Prayer, the Mightiest Force in the World,* says, "Everybody in every ordinary day has hundreds of chinks of idle wasted time which may be filled with flash prayers ten seconds or a minute long. Here are illustrations of such moments: upon awakening in the morning; in the bath; dressing; walking downstairs; asking the blessing at table; leaving the house; riding or walking to work; entering the elevator; between interviews; preparing for lunch; and a hundred more chinks all day long until crawling into bed and falling asleep."

We may pray as we travel. Many of us have found this to be an effective and thrilling way of intercession. We may pray for the one next to us or before us saying, "Lord, move into this life; show this person all that You have for him and bless him." We may pray as we read a newspaper. Lurid headlines and earth-shaking events may lead to intercession that the Lord of nations might have His will among men. The great personalities who determine the tides of history may be joined to Jesus Christ. It takes but a moment, the inner spirit lifted for a second from the printed page, "Lord Jesus, meet this man."

If we are sleepless in the night, we may pray. We may pray under the weight of our burdens and let them press us to God. The memories that flash into our minds may become the means of intercession. I may pray anywhere.

It is of value to consider *when* Jesus prayed. It is recorded that He arose a great while before daybreak and prayed. Like every devoted Hebrew, He had a morning watch, a quiet time in the early hours of the day when He sought His Father and communed with Him. I wonder what part of our day we give to God. Is it the fag end at night, when weary in mind and body and drooping in spirit, we yawn our requests to God? Or do we meet God in the morning before the day's activity has begun, when we are bright and fresh? The early meeting with God sanctifies the day and sensitizes us to our divine Companion who is with us through all its moments.

Jesus prayed before He ministered. Luke records that as Jesus presented Himself for His public ministry at the River Jordan, He was praying. All spiritual service begins in prayer.

Redemption is released through intercession. When we are hurled back in defeat from an objective clearly given of God, we may ask, "Was the fire-power of intercession first focused upon that point?" Without the power of God's Spirit released through prayer, the voice of our witness is like a child's cry lost in the raging tempest, and our efforts are like the pounding of a baby fist against granite walls. Through prayer, service is empowered.

Jesus prayed after He ministered (*Luke 5:15, 16*). Turning from the multitudinous duties of His day, He prayed. We need to pray after we serve that God may bring fruit from the seed which has been sown. He prayed before His great decisions. Proceeding to *Luke 6:12*, we learn that He continued all night in prayer before the choice of the twelve disciples. Do we pray earnestly before our great decisions, the decisions of vocation and location, the decisions of partnership and association? If every Christian man and woman prayed about their marriage before they came to the altar, our homes would be different and far happier.

Jesus prayed in times of crisis and need. He prayed in the Garden before His crucifixion (*Luke 22:39–44*). He prayed on the cross, ". . . Father, forgive them . . ." (*Luke 23:34*). His final utterance before death was a prayer (*Luke 23:46*), ". . . Father, into thy hands I commend my Spirit. . . ."

He taught ". . . that men ought always to pray, and not to faint" (*Luke 18:1*). So tomorrow, as you go to your office or shop and sit at your desk or stand at the bench, recognize God. It takes but a moment, the flash of a second, and the Lord walks in, and you are a partner with Him. As you, the busy housewife, go about your task, lift your heart to Christ. He is there. Let Him enter into your day with you, lead you

88

in His will and carry your concerns. Remember, everywhere and any time you can pray.

Let us now ask our Teacher *what* we should pray. The basic themes for prayer are best summarized by the Master in the Lord's Prayer, better called "The Disciples' Prayer." A lumberjack in the Northwoods found a New Testament. He began to read and became aware of his need of God. But he did not know how to pray. Then he came across the Lord's Prayer, cut it out and pasted it on the wall above his bunk. Just before retiring at night, he would point a stubby finger at the prayer and say, "Lord, them's my sentiments," and drop off to sleep. The lumberjack was not far from hitting the main point of prayer.

First there is the petition of worship. "Lord, may Thy Name be hallowed—made holy among men. Thy kingdom come. Thy will be done on earth as it is in heaven,"—three intercessory prayers for the name and purpose of God in the world. Then there are personal prayers—"Give us this day our daily bread" —our needs, "and forgive us our debts as we forgive our debtors"—a prayer for forgiveness. "Lead us not into temptation but deliver us from evil"—a request for guidance, and a final ascription of adoration, "For thine is the kingdom and the power and the glory forever."

Dr. Charles F. Whisten, authority on the Christian devotional life, has said that it is his practice to give every prospective bride and groom a copy of The Lord's Prayer on a small card, with the instructions to pray that prayer for one another often. The bride is counseled to pray for her husband, John. "Lord, may Thy Name be made holy in John's day. May Thy Kingdom come in him and through him today. May Thy will be done in his life and mine even as it is in heaven, perfectly.

Give him this day his daily bread, strength of body, wisdom of mind, fellowship of soul. Forgive him his sins, Lord, and grant him a truly forgiving spirit, even as I pray for forgiveness, for love and the power to be understanding and forgiving. Keep him from temptation. Deliver him from evil for Thine is the Kingdom and the power and the glory." If you do not know how to pray for one another, try this simple technique. Carry the card in your pocket and, as you drive along in your car, try praying The Lord's Prayer for loved ones, friends, and associates. If you are lying upon a sickbed, pray for others who are more sick than you are, the one in the hospital bed next to you, the one who comes to your mind now.

Jesus teaches that we are to pray for others. Did He not tell Simon, ". . . Simon, behold, Satan hath desired to have you, that he may sift you as wheat: But I have prayed for thee, that thy faith fail not . . ." (*Luke 22:31–32*). What new life and love would be released if we would faithfully follow His example.

We are to pray in the Name of Christ. "And whatsoever ye shall ask in my name, that will I do, that the Father may be glorified in the Son. If ye shall ask any thing in my name, I will do it" (*John 14:13, 14*). To pray in His Name means to pray for His concerns and cause, that what He came to do for us by His life, death, and resurrection may be fully accomplished. To pray in the Name of Christ is to appeal to God on the ground of Christ's merit, for His sake, and through His Person. It is asking largely and confidently of God because we are His through Christ.

> I know a soul that is steeped in sin,
> That no man's art can cure.

I know a Name
That can make that soul all pure.

I know a life that is lost to God,
Bound down by the things of earth.
I know a Name
That can bring that soul new birth.

I know of lands that are sunk in shame,
Of hearts that faint and tire.
But I know a Name
That can set these lands on fire.

A final question remains, *why* should we pray? Glancing at the pattern of prayer in the life of our Lord in Luke's Gospel, the answer is compelling. Why pray? Because prayer does things. As Jesus was praying, He was transfigured before His disciples. ". . . he took Peter and John and James, and went up into a mountain to pray. And as he prayed, the fashion of his countenance was altered, and his raiment became white and dazzling" (*Luke 9:28, 29*). In that sacred moment of intercession and communion, the deity of the Son of God shone through the garb of His humanity with ineffable glory. Think then, of the meaning of these words written to us. "But we all, with open face beholding as in a glass the glory of the Lord, are changed into the same image from glory to glory, even as by the Spirit of the Lord" (*II Corinthians 3:18*). Prayer is transforming. It brings man into the presence of the eternal and leaves the glow of God's glory upon his soul, the light of heaven in his heart.

As Jesus was praying, He was filled with the Holy Spirit and anointed for His mighty work. "Now when all the people were baptized, it came to pass, that Jesus also being baptized, and praying, the heaven was opened, And the Holy Ghost descended in a bodily shape like a dove upon him, and a voice came from heaven, which said, Thou art my beloved Son; in thee I am well pleased" (*Luke 3:21, 22*). So the Master teaches His followers "If ye then, being evil, know how to give good gifts unto your children; how much more shall your Heavenly Father give the Holy Spirit to them that ask him?" (*Luke 11: 13*). Before His disciples are sent into the world to bear witness to His Name, they are to tarry at Jerusalem in prayer until they are endued with power from on high. "And behold, I send the promise of my Father upon you: but tarry ye in the city of Jerusalem, until ye be endued with power from on high" (*Luke 24:49*). It was as the first Christians were praying that they were filled with the Holy Spirit at Pentecost and empowered for service.

> Lord, what a change within us, one short hour
> Spent in Thy presence will prevail to make,
> What heavy burdens from our bosoms take
> What parched grounds refresh as with a shower.
>
> We kneel, and all around us seems to lower;
> We rise, and all the distant and the near
> Stands forth in sunny outline, brave and clear.
> We kneel how weak; we rise, how full of power!
>
> Why should we ever weak or heartless be?
> Why are we ever overborne with care,
> Anxious or troubled, when with us is prayer

And joy and strength and courage are with Thee?
Archbishop Richard Chevenix Trench

Our Lord is stretched upon His face in the Garden of Geth-semane. He is engaged in an agony of intercession. Sweat as great drops of blood, falls to the ground. In prayer, He sur-renders Himself to the death of the cross for the redemption of the world. "Who in the days of his flesh, when he had of-fered up prayers and supplications with strong crying and tears unto him that was able to save him from death, and was heard in that he feared" (*Hebrews* 5:7). This prayer opened the tomb. Prayer raises the spiritually dead today. It quickens souls with new life in the Saviour. It enables the Holy Spirit to lead out into the light of God, redeemed souls released from sin and death, rejoicing in their Risen Lord.

Prayer thrusts our empty souls under the fountain of divine grace. Prayer opens the flood gates of divine life upon our barrenness. Prayer moves divine omnipotence to our weak-ness. Prayer brings God to man. Through prayer, God does the impossible. Then let us pray.

WHAT JESUS SAYS ABOUT THE TRUE HOME

For whosoever shall do the will of my Father which is in heaven, the same is my brother, and sister, and mother.

Matthew 12:50

HAPPY, HARMONIOUS, GODLY HOMES DO NOT SIMPLY HAPPEN. The attractive suburban house did not just fall into place. The lovely landscaping of the beautiful garden was not by accident. Behind it all was planning, purpose and intelligent labor. The owner first set down his needs and desires. Then he sought the help of an architect to shape up the plans, and a builder to execute them. He did not just dump the materials on a vacant lot and wait for them to form themselves into a house. No rational person would proceed that way. Yet the same family which gives thought and planning to the building of a house, will often give little thought to the building of a home for the glory of God. Then when a "jerry built" family structure begins to sag and totter because of conflicting wills and temperaments, even to the point sometimes of collapsing in ruin, the family will often pick themselves up from the rubble bewildered, embittered, and wondering why.

Should we leave to chance the most delicate and demanding of all human relationships, that of husband and wife, parents and children? The family demands the very best that purpose, plan, and intelligent effort can bring it. Above all, the home needs God and His grace.

An architect asked a young couple, "What type of a house do you desire?" The husband said, "Well . . ." and he was cut short. The wife took over and ventured, "We are not really very particular, but we would like the type of house that would go with a cute little door-knocker we picked up in Vermont last summer." But a true home is far bigger than a place to hang gadgets or to satisfy personal and petty desires. A true home is built for God and His glory. The will of God is to be the master plan for every family.

The Lord Jesus Christ is the Master Architect and Builder of homes. So let us give attention to His teaching on this subject.

Our Lord teaches that the true home is a window through which we may look up to the living God and through which the light of God may shine. Dr. Alfred E. Luccock tells us that in the first edition of Edith Wharton's novel, *The Age of Innocence*, she made a glaring mistake. She quotes what she supposes is the opening portion of the marriage service in the Prayer Book, but in reality it is the beginning of the burial service. Dr. Luccock goes on to say, "Too often marriage introduces lives into a sort of grave, without light or contact with the larger human family, shut up into selfish living. Altogether," he says, "there are too many homes that might have for their ceremony words like this: 'For as much as John and Mary have consented to holy matrimony we consign their bodies to a five-room tomb without windows on the world.'"

A house needs windows on the world and a home needs windows on God.

To convey the realities of God to us, the Lord has chosen as a favorite vehicle of thought the figure of the family. The deepest truths of the divine nature and purpose are expressed in terms of the home. God, Jesus says, is a Father. Repeatedly, this comes from His lips. "Our Father which art in heaven . . ." "If ye then, being evil, know how to give good gifts unto your children, how much more shall your Father which is in heaven give good things unto them that ask him?" (*Mat. 6:9; 7:11*). "Be ye therefore perfect, even as your Father which is in heaven is perfect" (*Mat. 5:48*). For the heart of God is a Father's heart and He desires to enter into relationship with us as His children. The Parable of the Prodigal Son, the greatest of all our Lord's parables, was taken right out of the context of the family. In the forgiveness of the returning prodigal, He enables us to understand the forgiveness of God for those who come to Him in repentance. Thus, the human family becomes a microcosm of the Kingdom of God.

He teaches us that one enters the Kingdom of God by spiritual birth. ". . . Except a man be born again, he cannot see the Kingdom of God" (*John 3:3*). Obviously, we receive our physical life through birth. Not one of us was ever in a position to bargain with our parents and say, "If you will make me a child, I will promise to be a good boy or girl all the time I am in your home." We may be appreciative and loving because of their gift of life and love, but we can never earn our relationship. So we are told by the Lord that we enter into the family of God by spiritual birth, a gracious gift received in Himself.

He also makes clear to us in His teaching, that sin is essentially a blow at a loving heart. The evil which curses humanity is our prodigal willfulness. We have chosen to go into a far country leaving the father's house, neglecting the father's purpose and plan and spurning His love. Sin in its essence is a clenched fist of rebellion thrust into the face of the Father in heaven. Likewise, He teaches us that forgiveness and fellowship are not to be had through a process of legal regulations but through reconciliation. "For God so loved the world that he gave his only begotten Son . . ." (*John 3:16*). He seeks us with marvelous self-giving love. Not only like the Prodigal's father, does He see us a great way off and run to welcome us, but He reaches us in the far country and stirs us to return to Him. He Himself has provided that redeeming grace which bridges the chasm between ourselves and His holy life. He has come in the Person of Jesus Christ to lift the prodigal race to His heart by means of the cross. He makes clear that the supreme law of life is love, love which is self-giving and not self-seeking. This is the way He responds to us. It is important to note that Jesus teaches us these tremendous truths about the Father not only by declaration but by demonstration— more by what He does than by what He says. The lasting lessons of life are learned through example rather than precept. It is easy to forget what we learn in the classroom, but what is learned in the context of the family abides. Our children catch more from our actions than from our instructions.

"The mother of Sir Walter Scott was a lover of poetry and art. The mother of Lord Byron was proud, ill-tempered, and violent. The mother of Napoleon Bonaparte was full of ambition and energy. The mother of Lord Bacon was a woman of superior mind and deep piety. The mother of George Washington was a fine and good woman. The mother of Patrick Henry was eloquent in speech. The mother of John and

Charles Wesley was pious and filled with executive ability. The mother of Philip Doddridge taught him the Scriptures from the Dutch tiles on the fireplace. The lives of these women gave content to their words, and direction to the lives and minds they were molding. These men all walked in the steps of their mothers. So it is with our children.

Our Heavenly Father teaches His children not only by word, but by deed. "Hereby perceive we the love of God, because he laid down his life for us: and we ought to lay down our lives for the brethren." "My little children, let us not love in word, neither in tongue; but in deed and in truth" (*I John 3:16, 18*). Through the marvelous self-giving of Christ, we learn the nature of real love.

We cannot fully calculate the transforming power of this life of Christ. For example, His attitude toward women in the gospels has brought emancipation to womanhood wherever the gospel is known, and crowned her with dignity and honor. He said of marriage, "What God hath joined together, let no man put asunder" and wherever He is recognized, marriage becomes a spiritual union in God. He has touched and transformed childhood. He brought a little child and set him in the midst of the disciples. Ever since that time, wherever Jesus has been known, the little child has been the center of love and concern.

Perhaps we do not fully appreciate the difference between the Christian and the pagan view of childhood. The radical change Christianity brought may be illustrated by a papyrus letter which recently has been uncovered. Written by a soldier to his wife back in Rome, the letter was dated about the year 1 A.D.—about the time Christ Himself was a baby. It reads, "We are still in Alexandria. I beg you to look after the child and as soon as we get wages I will send you something." Many a letter starts like that today! But this is the point—the letter continues, "If it is a boy, let it live. If it is a girl, throw it away!" In those days the Roman father had the right to take every baby in his hands, and if deformed, weak, or unwanted, he would break its back and throw it away. But Christ did something to that calloused world. He gathered the little children in His arms and said, "Of such is the Kingdom of Heaven." Ever since, His followers have seen children through His eyes.

Let us see what Christ has done to love. He has shown us that love is the greatest thing in the world and that the nature of real love is self-giving. "Greater love hath no man than this, that a man lay down his life for his friends" (*John 15:13*).

This needs to be emphasized today when our ideas of love are so highly colored by that which comes from Hollywood and the contemporary novels. In an article entitled "The Romantic Road to Divorce," Denis de Rougement says: "The type of love upon which a great many marriages are founded is a fever, generally light and considered infinitely interesting to contract. This, the Anglo-Saxon calls romance. We are in the act of trying it out and miserably failing at it. One of the most pathological experiments a civilized society has ever imagined is the basing of marriage—which is lasting—upon romance, which is a passing fancy. It is clear that in speaking of romance we have not been speaking of love in general, but of certain aspects of love which our era cultivates and which, too often, are accepted as love itself." One of the greatest delusions of our day is the false, superficial and dangerous idea about the nature of love. Jesus shows us what love really is. He has defined it and demonstrated it. Writing to the

99

Christian family, the Apostle Paul said, "Husbands, love your wives, even as Christ also loved the church, and gave himself for it" (*Eph.* 5:25).

It is my privilege to counsel with those preparing for marriage. I endeavor to give them one sure guide for every human relationship in the home, a key which will be the solution to any problem. Let them love one another and respond to one another as God in Christ has loved them. How has God treated me in my indifference, my willfulness, my failure, my ingratitude? He continues to remain the lover of my soul. How has Christ treated me when I have been unfaithful to Him, when I have rushed through my days without thinking of Him, when I have had no room in my heart for Him? Is He through with me? Does He turn His back and walk away from me? No! He is there to forgive me, to reach down and under and lift me in love to His own great heart. Let me remember how God treats me in Christ and I will understand how I am to love.

There is a story concerning an old philosopher of Greece. On one occasion his wife gave him a severe tongue lashing. He listened in silence which only infuriated her the more, so she took a bucket of cold water and threw it at him. Though drenched from head to foot, very calmly and philosophically he remarked, "After that thunder and lightning storm I rather expected a shower." God does not treat us philosophically. He does not bear with us in a detached way. He moves toward the point of our need and there He lovingly gives Himself to us. Oh, that every home and every heart had a window on God, and looking through it into the face of Jesus Christ, would see how families are to live!

A successful man in the community appeared at the home

of a doctor friend. In obvious distress, he cried, "My car is packed. I'm leaving home. I'm through! I have done everything I know how and it just won't work." The doctor asked him to sit down. "Don't be a fool," he said. "Leaving your wife and family is not the way out." "Well," the man replied, "I have tried everything I know and there seems no way to get along." The doctor said, "I want you to try one more thing and if that fails, I have nothing more to say. I want you to go back to your home, say to your wife, 'Dear, let's pray together.' Then go into your bedroom, close the door and kneel down together. Pray to God and in the name of Christ, tell Him that you have sinned against Him and against your wife in that you have not loved her as He loves her. Moreover, you have done this and this and this and contributed to your problem." He continued, "Don't mention her mistakes and failures to God. Tell Him about your own and ask Him to fill your life with His kind of love for her." There was a window opened in that home and it brought the light and love of God.

I trust that your home is not a five-roomed tomb without windows on God. Rather swing wide the portals toward Christ and order your home in the light of His love.

The home is not only a window on God giving us light, but it is also a doorway through which He enters the life.

It is a source of unceasing wonder to me that when the infinite God became incarnate and walked among men in order that He might be joined with us forever, He entered through the low portal of a Nazareth home and was born a baby in Bethlehem. God came into the world through a home. It was the doorway of His deity in flesh. But there is another amazing miracle. Jesus Christ will come into our hearts and homes today. He calls, "Behold, I stand at the door, and knock: if any man hear my voice, and open the door, I will come in to him, and will sup with him, and he with me" (*Rev. 3:20*). "Oh," someone says, "There you go again veering off on the mystical and emotional. I don't believe that God does this sort of thing." May I ask this question? If you were to hear a knock on your door this afternoon and glancing out the window, saw one who looked like Jesus Christ, would you eagerly welcome Him into your family and home? You say, "What has that to do with it? I just said I don't believe this sort of thing happens." I know you said that, but would you like Christ in your home if He *should* knock at your door? To me, this is the crucial question. Are we ready to make room for Him? Do we want His way of living in the home? Are we willing to acknowledge Him as Lord of the family and of the heart. If so, be assured He is truly knocking and the moment He is given a real, definite invitation from an earnest life, He is there.

I recently called on a couple in our community who had two lovely children. They said to me quite frankly, "I guess there is something wrong with our religion. We have the form of it but not the substance. It does not seem to click and there is no reality in our lives." As we talked a little further I explained to them that God stands ready to enter any life and any home that really wants Him. We turned to the Scriptures and read, "Behold I stand at the door and knock . . ." (*Rev. 3:20*).

Addressing the husband and wife, I said, "Would you really like Jesus Christ not only to be the guest of this household, but its Lord and Saviour?" "Yes, we really would," they both replied. The three of us knelt together and directly and simply they invited Jesus Christ first into their hearts and then into their home. When I left, I could tell by the firmness with

102

which they gripped my hand and by the new light in their eyes that God was there in new reality. Prayer in the home opens the door to God. He steps into the midst of the family with new power as its members pray together.

The Bible is another doorway to God. His Word in the heart of a Christian family is the source of America's greatness. God dwells in the home where parents share the things of God with their children, teach them to turn to Him in prayer, to trust Him as "the way, the truth, and the life" and guide them in ordering their lives according to His will. Such a home has an eternal foundation and abides forever.

I had a home like this. My parents not only taught me the things of Christ, but lived them before me. I vividly remember my father leading the family in daily devotions about the table. He would read a few verses of Scripture from the well-worn Bible, explain them, apply them to our lives, and conclude with prayer. An oft repeated prayer remains with me to this hour, "Lord, grant to us in that great day that we may be an unbroken circle about thy throne." Into my childish mind there came an awareness that the love and fellowship of our home would last forever. This prayer follows me today. May Christ give us all a true home centered in Him.

WHAT JESUS SAYS ABOUT LIFE'S
MAIN BUSINESS

*But seek first the kingdom of God, and his righteous-
ness; and all these things shall be added unto you.*

Matthew 6:33

WHAT IS THE MAIN BUSINESS OF LIFE? A QUESTION WILL BRING
the matter quickly before us. "What is your vocation, that
which you consider your main job or occupation?" Your reply
may be, "I am a clerk, an engineer, a mechanic, a nurse, a
teacher. I am a business man, a professional man, a student."
"Mine," another adds, "is the most difficult and demanding of
all vocations. I am a housewife, a mother."

Let us ask another question. "Are you a Christian? Have
you acknowledged Jesus Christ as Saviour and Lord? Have
you received His new life within?" If so, your true vocation is
not business or medicine or engineering or keeping house.
These are but your avocation, your subordinate occupation.
Your real call and highest summons is the will of God. The
Christian's main business in life is to be about his Heavenly
Father's business. Our Lord makes this very clear and leaves

no room for equivocation. "But seek ye first the kingdom of God and his righteousness . . ." (*Mat. 6:33*).

This must have been disturbing to the disciples. All their lives they had labored to earn a living. Their livelihood was a controlling concern and now the Master teaches them, "Therefore do not be anxious, saying, 'What shall we eat?' or 'What shall we drink?' or 'What shall we wear?' For the Gentiles seek all these things; and your heavenly Father knows that you need them all. But seek first his kingdom and his righteousness, and all these things shall be yours as well" (*Mat. 6:31–33, RSV*). Or as Phillips translates the verses, "Set your hearts on His Kingdom and His goodness, and all these things will come to you as a matter of course." Those who respond to the call of Christ have one vocation, one major occupation—to set their hearts on God's kingdom and goodness.

Many Christians today are suffering from a tragic divorce. In their thinking, life has been separated into two mutually exclusive areas—the sacred and the secular. These are viewed as incompatible. They are felt to require two different sets of actions. There are sacred acts such as prayer, Bible reading, worship, service in the church, and the other acts which spring directly from faith. Over and against these sacred acts are the secular ones, the sort of thing that everyone is always doing—eating, sleeping, working, and performing dull duties of the daily round. These are mistakenly regarded as without any spiritual value and are often performed grudgingly, because so much of our time is devoted to them. On the Lord's Day, we arise and put on our "Sunday best," saying to ourselves, "Today will be sacred and spiritual. Today I can worship and serve the Lord." But Monday finds us putting on our overalls or business suit in a depressed frame of mind saying, "Today

I have to mess around in worldly things and serve the devil. If only I were a minister or missionary, I could perform some truly spiritual service and attain a truly spiritual life."

But this divorce is utterly wrong. God does not cut up and partition life into the sacred and the secular. "What therefore God hath joined together, let not man put asunder" (*Mat. 19:6*). The man at the shop or office must have the same sense of mission as the man behind the pulpit. The teacher of children in a grade school may render as sacred a service to Jesus Christ as the teacher in the Sunday School. The soul is not sanctified by devotion to a few specialized activities in full-time Christian service. The soul is sanctified by the dedication of the whole life to God and His will.

During the last World War, thousands of bombing planes were sent on missions of destruction. After the war, a few of them were taken over for commercial service. They are called "converted bombers." A converted bomber is the same plane that once carried a lethal load of destruction. It has the same wings and fuselage, the same type motors, the same cockpit and instrument panel. The bomb racks are gone. The gun turret is gone. It has a new paint job, but it is essentially the same plane. It has however, this difference. It has a new owner. It carries new cargo. It has a new pilot. This is true conversion.

In Christian conversion, Jesus Christ delivers us from the old life and possesses us for God. He enters into the cockpit of the heart, takes over the controls and operates the old life on a new course, pointing us to a new and glorious purpose— ". . . the kingdom of God and his righteousness. . . ." This means, of course, that all our relationships and activities are to be converted and viewed now in the light of our new mission. The old job, the old routine of the day, the old cargo which remains to be carried, may be lifted through Jesus Christ and moved toward God. The spiritual may invade and take over the secular through a new purpose by the power of Jesus Christ. Do you want to venture on a sacred mission and serve an eternal cause? Then turn over the controls to Jesus Christ. Recognize the fact that you belong utterly to God. Then start operating your home, your business, your job with your heart set on God's Kingdom and His goodness.

Our Lord did not divorce the sacred and the secular. Observe how all in His life was devoted to the Father and ordered by one dominating purpose, to "seek . . . first the kingdom of God. . . ." Until He was thirty years of age, He labored quietly in an obscure carpentry shop in Nazareth. He was not less consecrated or spiritual behind the bench at Nazareth than He was teaching the throngs in the temple at Jerusalem. He was not less sanctified in breaking the bread to feed the five thousand than when He preached to them the everlasting gospel and fed their souls. He was not less loving and spiritual healing the sick or stooping to wash the disciples' feet than when He was praying in the Garden of Gethsemane. No, every phase and every act of His life was performed as unto the Father. All of life was God's.

By working with His hands in the shop at Nazareth, Jesus teaches us that we may handle a hammer or a piece of wood to the glory of God. The common duties of life may be sanctified, ennobled by performing them in the light of our high calling in God. The crucial factor is not the nature of our daily task as much as the nature of our purpose; not the name of our secular vocation but the nature of our spiritual vision; not where we find ourselves at work but what we do with our work and why.

Moreover, in the mind of Jesus there is no divorce between professional and amateur Christians, between clergy and laity, as though one group is serving God all the time and the other group only part of the time. Jesus Christ conscripts all of the time of all His followers. We simply serve God in different ways and with different responsibilities. Why is it that only ministers and missionaries are supposed to have a definite call of God for their service? Every Christian is on a divine mission. Every believer is an ambassador of God. Dr. D. Elton Trueblood in his book, *Your Other Vocation,* makes a strong appeal to rouse every Christian to enter into his high calling in Christ. He contrasts the Church at Corinth in the year 52 A.D. with the First Church of Technopolis in 1953. In the modern church there are members and ministers. The members engage the ministers to do the preaching, to expound the Scriptures, to call on the people in the neighborhood. A staff is secured in some instances to carry on the many functions of church life, but the member often merely sits like a spectator at a ball game, letting the professionals conduct the show. The Church at Corinth stands in sharp contrast. To begin with, there was no church building. The congregation met in private homes. There were no professional ministers. Every member served his brother. There were no full-time preachers. All preached the gospel at every opportunity. There was no one employed to visit and make calls. All went about their community, serving in love and sharing the good news. That Church had power and a burning love for God and man. Every Christian viewed his home, his work, his fellow man as a divine ministry and entered it with joy.

The late John R. Mott, himself a powerful example of what the lay minister can be, has described the universal ministry of the early church in memorable words. "The disciple discussed with his teacher and fellow-students, the Christian truth which had laid powerful hold upon him. The slave who had fallen under the spell of the One who had come to proclaim release to captives, could not refrain from pointing to the great Deliverer. Wherever the Christian disciples scattered, the evidences of Christianity multiplied, working quietly as a leaven, for the conversion of one household after another. It is this commending by life and word, the reality and wonder working of the living Lord on the part of the rank and file of His disciples, within the sphere of their daily calling that best explains the penetration of Roman society with the world-conquering gospel."

If the Church at Technopolis in our day were to match the same mission and dedication of the Church of Corinth in its day, it too could turn the world upside down.

In the past thirty-five years, communism has swept over a third of the inhabited globe. The thrust of the advance has not been the logic of communism's ideology, but the totality of demand and dedication of life upon its followers. As I see it, the crucial issue of this twentieth century in the struggle for the loyalties of mankind, is whether Christians will bring to Jesus Christ the same measure of practical dedication to the job that millions of Communists are bringing to the cause of Karl Marx. If we would, nothing could stand against the transforming impact of a triumphant Church.

Our Lord, in His great commission commanded, ". . . Go ye into all the world, and preach the gospel to every creature" (*Mark 16:15*). He meant that extensively. We are to carry the saving word to all people, all nations, all races, everywhere. But He also meant the commission to be taken intensively. We are to carry His gospel into the world of education, of commerce, industry, agriculture, culture, and art. His disciple is not to separate from the common life around him, but to penetrate it and transform it for God by the power of the gospel. There are opportunities open to the layman which are closed to the minister. The layman has a position among his daily associates impossible for the minister to attain. The layman's amateur standing is a great advantage. People expect ministers to say and do certain things and are braced to withstand them. Your genuine Christian life, your loving friendship, your spontaneous witness to the grace of God as a layman, carry a far more effective and convincing demonstration of the reality of the Saviour than the most eloquent sermon. The Great Commission is directed as much to the layman as the minister. The layman too, has a field of service. Some are called to be ministers of the church, but all are called to a ministry in Christ.

If you think that the service of God is something where men are separated from ordinary occupations, then listen to what is written of the Apostle Paul. "Because he was of the same craft, he abode with them, and wrought: for by their occupation they were tentmakers" (*Acts 18:3*). Tentmaking was a laborious trade, not highly esteemed and poorly paid. Yet the Apostle Paul earned his way making tents and used the hours of labor to share with Aquila and Priscilla the truth and life of Jesus Christ.

Francis of Assisi was a soldier. John Bunyon was a tinker. John Woolman was a tailor. Charles Finney was a lawyer. D. L. Moody was a shoe-clerk, a salesman. The two men, perhaps most used in the last generation to advance the cause of the world mission of Christ were both laymen—John R. Mott and Robert E. Speer. Who can calculate the influence for God as President Eisenhower, a Christian layman, bowed his head to pray before his Inaugural Address. What a pulpit! How moving was the message. Our main business then as Christians is to be about the Father's business, to seek first the Kingdom of God in our personal lives, doing His will right where we are.

We are also to seek the Kingdom of God in our occupational lives. In New Testament times, the slave was treated as human chattel, bound in soul-destroying servitude, without rights or privileges. His day was a round of dull drudgery. But Jesus Christ set the spirit of the slave free and brought dignity to his work, transforming it into sacramental service. "Slaves, obey your human masters sincerely with a proper sense of respect and responsibility, as service rendered to Christ Himself; not with the idea of currying favour with men, but as the servants of Christ conscientiously doing what you believe to be the will of God for you. You may be sure that God will reward a man for good work, irrespectively of whether the man be slave or free" (*Ephesians 6:5–8, Phillips*).

One may go to work at times, feeling like a slave, bound to dreary, meaningless duties. But he can perform that work for the Lord, knowing that He will be pleased with faithful, conscientious work whatever may be the recognition of others. The added touch given to trivialities because of devotion to Jesus Christ, can make an ordinary task shine with the glory of God.

But let us be careful to avoid trivial or harmful employment. John Oliver Nelson has said, "Almighty God doesn't call any man or woman to a trivial or unimportant life work. If you can't see your job as being somehow vital and meaningful to mankind, change it or get out of it. We cannot seek the Kingdom of God in things which are harmful.

Nearly every type of work brings with it contacts with other human beings. Each contact is a door to Christian opportunity. Each person may become an object of Christian ministry. Do I see my boss merely as an employer or as the one for whom the Supervisor of heaven has a plan and divine purpose? Do I view men and women as customers or as persons loved of the Lord? Do I think of men merely as employees or those whom I may serve even as the Son of God serves me? Each person is a parish, each man a mission field, each individual a divine opportunity.

I know a business man whose day at the office begins with a prayer acknowledging God as the Senior Partner of the corporation. I know a school teacher who walks down the corridor to the classroom relying on Christ to teach His truth through her life and love. I know a doctor who calls in the Great Physician on every case to help heal the body and soul of his patient. I know a housewife who asks the Lord to have His way in her heart and in those of her household as she moves through the duties of the day. These all say, "Lord, I am Thy servant. Help me to do this work for Thee today."

My place in life must be occupied by moral power. Small though my influence may be, I must stand for the right. I must be "the salt of the earth . . . the light of the world." Industry today calls for integrity. The commercial world must have character; professional life, purity and selfless purpose. Wherever the Lord places me I must be "salt" and "light."

But my highest spiritual service is to bring myself to God.

"I appeal to you therefore, brethren, by the mercies of God, to present your bodies as a living sacrifice, holy and acceptable to God, which is your spiritual worship" (*Romans 12:1, RSV*). Anywhere, at any time, I seek first the Kingdom of God and His righteousness when I respond with all that I am and have, to all that I know of Jesus Christ.

> A charge to keep I have,
> A God to glorify;
> A never-dying soul to save,
> And fit it for the sky.
>
> To serve the present age,
> My calling to fulfill;
> O may it all my powers engage,
> To do my Master's will.
>
> Arm me with jealous care,
> As in Thy sight to live,
> And O, Thy servant, Lord, prepare,
> A strict account to give!
>
> (Charles Wesley)

Yes, my main business in life is my Father's business.

WHAT JESUS SAYS ABOUT HIS PLAN
FOR THE WORLD

*Jesus saith unto him, Thou hast said: nevertheless I say
unto you, Hereafter shall ye see the Son of man sitting on
the right hand of power, and coming in the clouds of
heaven.*

Matthew 26:64

In the gospels the theme, "The Kingdom of God," occurs
well over a hundred times. It is not only the subject of the first
address given by our Lord in the gospels, but it is the theme
of His last message to the disciples. It is recorded that, after
His resurrection from the dead, He spoke to them of things
concerning the Kingdom of God.

The note is sounded all through His ministry. How many of
His parables begin "... The Kingdom of God is like unto...."
He sent His disciples out into the villages of Israel to proclaim
"the Kingdom of God." Indeed, He teaches us that this is to
be the goal, the main objective of life. "But seek ye first the
kingdom of God, and his righteousness; and all these things
shall be added unto you" (*Mat. 6:33*). He taught us thus to
pray: "Our Father which art in heaven, hallowed be thy

114

Name. Thy Kingdom come. Thy will be done on earth as it is in heaven. . . ." It is the watchword of the gospel of Christ. It is the master thought of the Master Teacher.

But Jesus did more than point us to the Kingdom of God. He presented Himself as the King. Let us go back in our thinking to that occasion when crowds thronged the narrow streets of Jerusalem, excited and eager with anticipation. Soon they caught sight of a band of men pushing through the multitude, escorting a Figure riding upon an ass. A tremendous shout of welcome reverberates through the narrow streets. It changes from a shout to a loud chant, a refrain which is caught up and repeated again and again by the people. ". . . Blessed be the king that cometh in the name of the Lord. . . ."

Jesus Christ rode into Jerusalem, deliberately presenting Himself to the people as their Messiah, the rightful Ruler and Lord. So it is that Jesus Christ presents Himself to all people everywhere, in every age, as King and Lord of all. During the trial of Jesus, Pilate, the Roman governor, leaned forward in his chair, endeavoring to penetrate into the mind of the Man before him. "Art thou a king then?" The answer is forthright and definite. "Thou sayest that I am a king. . . ." Or, as we would say, "You are entirely right. That is what I am."

The Sanhedrin, seeking to find some pretext to put Him to death, called upon Him to answer an oath, "Art thou the Messiah of God?" And our Lord again answers positively, "Thou sayest." That is right. ". . . Hereafter shall ye see the Son of man sitting on the right hand of power, and coming in the clouds of heaven" (*Mat. 26:64*). He is a King not only on this terrestrial sphere, but He is the King of Glory over an eternal domain. This is the majestic claim of Jesus Christ. He placed within the hearts of His followers not only a fervent hope, but a burning conviction that at the end of time the high arches of glory would ring to the triumphant shout, ". . . The Kingdoms of this world are become the Kingdoms of our Lord, and of his Christ; and he shall reign for ever and ever" (*Rev. 11:15*).

According to the Bible, humanity is under a blight of rebellion against its Maker and rightful Lord. Humanity knows moral ruin because of a moral revolt against God. God is meant to be the Lord of life, but man has placed his own will in supremacy. We are a runaway world from God, the sole and rightful Lord of all.

Hear the words which Lord Byron puts into the mouth of Satan, "He that does not bow the knee to God has already bowed to me." And this is the supreme tragedy of mankind.

In the early days of astronomy, the earth was conceived to be the center of the universe, and all the stars revolved around the earth. But the Ptolemaic system did not work. Then man discovered with Copernicus that the earth was not the center of the universe, but that the solar system revolved about the sun. Thus we are solar-centric and not geo-centric. When man proceeded upon that truth, he found that his problems worked out and the sums added up. If things do not add up to make sense today, whether we look on the world around us or experience within us, it is fundamentally because man has chosen to revolve around himself. He has put himself at the center and ignored the Son of Righteousness, who is the true Center of the orbit of our being. Jesus has come to restore a runaway race to its rightful Ruler. He purposes by the power of His redeeming love to break down the resistance of the human will, to capture our hearts and renew them by His

Spirit, to swing us into God and His will, which is the true orbit of life.

Christ was not a pessimist. He did not fear that humanity would end in some monstrous tragedy. He did not think humanity's last chapter would be nothing but extinction and ruin. The end of time in the mind of Christ is the Throne of God, supreme over all creatures everywhere, the redeemed people of God renewed in glory serving Him in freedom and joy forever. To this glorious goal He gives Himself. For this, He touches our lives with His scepter and calls for our allegiance.

Let us consider briefly what Christ has to say about the nature of this Kingdom. He teaches that the Kingdom commences with the rule of God in the heart. The patriotic Israelite sought earnestly for a political kingdom, a national state. He hoped sometime, that the glory of the Davidic Kingdom would be restored. He looked for a king who, by the power of sword and scepter, would cast out the Roman oppressor and establish a Jewish domain. But the Kingdom of God, Jesus teaches, is not nationalistic but moral. It is brought to pass not by the power of men exerted from without, but by the new life of God growing from within. The real oppressor is not Caesar but Satan. The army to be feared and fought is not an army encased in armor and bearing swords, but the spiritual army of evil which invades the sanctities of the soul. Moreover, God's Kingdom begins in the secret places within, an order of goodness, humility, and love.

Jesus is a different kind of King. He comes riding on the humble ass. He takes the cross for His throne and rules by self-giving love. He has a different kind of kingdom and different kinds of subjects whose allegiance comes from within.

117

I saw the conquerors riding by
With cruel lips and faces wan.
Musing the kingdoms sacked and burned
Arose the Mongol, Genghis Khan.

And Alexander like a god
Who sought to weld this world in one,
And Caesar with his laurel wreath
And like a thing from hell, the Hun.

Then, all they perished from the earth
As fleeting shadows from a glass,
And conquering down the centuries
Came Christ, the swordless, on an ass.

The Conquerors—Harry Kemp

We have had enough of earthly kings. We have seen enough of the tyranny and oppression of temporal power. We need a King who reigns within the heart in righteousness and love.

Our Lord teaches that the rule of God in the world is spiritual and not material. Beginning at the center, He creates a new man with new allegiance and new motivation. This new man in turn exerts a new influence in the home, in society, and upon the world. Dr. Herman Melville Horn of New York University has this significant paragraph in his book, *The Philosophy of Christian Education:*

> Social systems, ideal commonwealths have been given the world by many paper reformers. Plato's *Republic;* Sir Thomas More's *Utopia;* Francis Bacon's *New Atlantis* and others. Perhaps we should include in this the volume of Karl Marx on *Capital.* Of all these Plato and

Marx have been most influential. To most of them the words of Tennyson apply.

> Our little systems have their day,
> They have their day and cease to be.

Now the paradox. Jesus, without a social system, has been more influential in reshaping society than these with a social system. The reason? Because He gives society a conscience which transforms society. Because He changes the lives of individuals and they in turn change the life of society. Because He provides the dynamic to change society. Because He begins with the means, the new man, and the new man leads to the end, the new society . . . and behold, the astonishing results of His method.

The Kingdom of God, Jesus taught, is social and not solitary. It begins with the new man redeemed through Jesus Christ. The new man is placed in a new society of redeemed people. There is now a new fellowship, the family of God, in which all, related to the one Father, are brothers and sisters. This is a new kind of organism Christ's Body of which He is the Head, formed into a living thing by His Spirit. It is a new order of humanity, a redeemed society, the fellowship of God's people on earth.

Society today is desperately searching for community. It has been endeavoring to live without God and has found life empty and lonely. A little boy, running away from home, enjoys his new liberty when the day is bright, but, when the shadows lengthen, he knows an unutterable loneliness and longs to be home once again. So men are longing for their true home, but, apart from God, they have not been able to find it.

Napoleon said to his people, "Make the nation your home —La Patrie and its glory!" But his plan ended in bloodshed and disillusionment. Adolph Hitler shouted, "Let the bond be that of blood and race!" But that philosophy, too, ended in destruction. There are prophets today who say, "The true community of life is economic." But this dictatorship of a soulless society will also fail and fall. There is only one communion that will ever give true fellowship. This is the Church of Jesus Christ, composed of those who have been humbled at the cross and made aware of their need, who are grateful for divine grace, rich in divine love, sharing a common Lord, a common life, and a common destiny.

> Blest be the tie that binds,
> Our hearts in Christian love.

The Kingdom, Jesus teaches, is universal, not local. From the very beginning of His ministry, He talked in these terms. He said, "The field is the world. . . ." "Ye are the salt of the earth. . . ." "Ye are the light of the world." This expectation of a universal rule is one of the evidences of Jesus' deity. How does it happen that a man who began as a carpenter in an obscure village in a small province of the Roman Empire dared to envision, to labor and give Himself for a worldwide Kingdom? Jesus spoke of His reign being for all classes, all peoples, all races, all ages—a universal domain. His great commission directed His disciples to "every creature" and to "all nations." He would bind the world to the throne of God.

There has always been an attractive power in big things. Alexander the Great dreamed of an empire that would stretch

from the Mediterranean to India, and he inspired his followers with fanatical zeal. Adolph Hitler conjured a super-race
reigning a thousand years over all the peoples of earth, and
young men arose by the millions to fight and die for that
dream. Karl Marx, in his frustration, conceived a classless
world society, and his demand of total dedication to the concept has grown into near realization in a third of the globe.
One of the strong appeals of communism today is the vastness
of its vision. It seeks to change the world.

Jesus Christ has a greater plan than this. No military genius,
no power-drunk dictator, no dreaming idealist ever conceived
as bold a plan or mapped as daring a campaign as the Man of
Nazareth. He stood before His disciples, a handful of ordinary men from the common walks of life, arrayed against the
hostile world and commanded, "Go ye therefore and teach
all nations . . . teaching them to observe all things whatsoever
I have commanded you; and lo, I am with you alway . . ."

> Jesus shall reign where'er the sun
> Doth his successive journeys run;
> His kingdom stretch from shore to shore,
> Till moons shall wax and wane no more.

The Kingdom of our Lord is not only universal; it is total.
There are no areas to which He does not lay claim. He does
not divide things between the sacred and the secular, saying,
"This is God's and this is man's; this is spiritual and this is
material." Jesus draws a circle around the whole of life,
touches it with His scepter, and says, "This is mine."

Some would have us believe that social questions are outside the province of religion. "Preach religion" they insist.
"Stay out of the social issues and politics." But when Jesus

Christ entered Jerusalem, He entered the heart of the national life, and He rode on the hard streets where the people lived. He came as King to the city and nation as well as Lord to the temple.

We of the Calvinist tradition love the phrase, "sovereignty of God." Its meaning is that God has a perfect will for all of life and that Jesus Christ is Lord of all. Nothing is to be restricted from His reign. No one is to say to Christ, "This far you may come but no farther. This much you may have but no more." The Kingdom of God is total. The reign of Christ is to be complete. Let us be sure that every area of life and experience is surrendered to His rule, that we do not presume to set limits to His domain.

Though it has already begun, the Kingdom awaits a final consummation. It is both present and future; present in that wherever Christ is Lord, the Kingdom exists, and future in that it awaits a glorious day of consummation. ". . . Hereafter shall ye see the Son of man sitting on the right hand of power, and coming in the clouds of heaven." It was this specific claim of Jesus which caused the Sanhedrin to condemn Him. They arose in rage, rent their robes, and said, "He is guilty of death."

But He is coming again, and ". . . The kingdoms of this world are become the kingdoms of our Lord, and of His Christ . . ." (*Rev. 11:15*). ". . . at the name of Jesus every knee should bow . . . and that every tongue should confess that Jesus Christ is Lord . . ." (*Phil. 2:10, 11*). ". . . He shall not fail nor be discouraged, till he have set judgment in the earth: and the isles shall wait for his law" (*Isaiah 42:4*).

He is coming again! What happened on the streets of Jerusalem—the palm branches and the glad shouts of welcome—is just a faint foregleam of that which will break in upon the world of men when Christ the Lord shall return in power to reign.

We do not face the future with fear. We do not enter tomorrow in a cloud of uncertainty, even in this atomic age with all its terrors. The victory has already been won. He who overcame evil and conquered death by His resurrection and ascension will return, and His victory shall be complete.

> Lead on, O King Eternal
> We follow, not with fears,
> For gladness breaks like morning
> Where'er Thy face appears.
> Thy cross is lifted o'er us;
> We journey in its light;
> The crown awaits the conquest;
> Lead on, O God of might!

It's thrilling to be Christ's! What an exultant note of joy sings in our hearts when we know that we move to final, complete, and glorious victory in that day of His revealing! Meanwhile, in its light we labor, and in its certainty we live.

But of all the glorious aspects of His Kingdom, most wonderful of all is that God rules in grace and infinite love. Napoleon at St. Helena turned to Count Montholan with the inquiry, "Can you tell me who Jesus Christ was?" The question was declined. Napoleon proceeded, "I will tell you. Alexander, Caesar, Charlemagne, and I have founded great empires, but upon what did these creations of our genius depend? Upon force. Jesus Christ alone founded His empire upon love and to this very day, millions will die for Him."

Christ makes us citizens and servants of God by capturing

our hearts. He binds us to Himself, not by the scourge of the whip, not with the blade of the sword, not with the chain of the captive, but by love. This King has come from glory, laid aside His robes of authority, and garbed Himself with human nature. He moved down to the low levels of our need and suffered with us and for us. He made the cruel reed His scepter and the crown of thorns His diadem; He chose the cross for His throne that He might win us by His love. When we have received His forgiveness—rebels that we are to the will of God—there comes an instant desire, a consuming passion to live for Him and to do His will.

It is right that we should give ourselves to Him. He alone is worthy. He alone is good enough and kind enough to rule the human will. He has purchased our lives by the giving of His own. When we surrender to Christ the King and trust Him, we enter the realm of God and experience His gracious rule.

I remember having lunch with a young man some years ago. He was an instructor at the University of California, studying for his doctorate. As we sat in the Faculty Club and talked over some personal problems, he said to me with an air of wistfulness, "I was reared in a Christian home, but the Christian faith has become unreal to me. God is not much more than a philosophical concept." We talked further and I asked, "Why don't you venture this? If you feel that Jesus Christ is the highest and best you know in life, if you sense that God has done a redeeming work for you and that His love reaches you, why don't you authorize Christ to come into your life as King? Why don't you open every door and surrender yourself to Him?" By this time, the others had gone, and we were almost alone. With moist eyes, he bowed his head at the luncheon table and simply said, "Christ, I open the door to You. Too long I have kept You, my King, outside. Come into my heart. Redeem it from its selfishness and sin. Remove its fears and its conflicts. Reign forever as my rightful Lord."

The following week several young people from his class came to me with bright faces, saying, "We spent an hour with our instructor today and he spent the whole time telling us what Jesus Christ means to him. He told us that Christ is a real Lord and He has a real Kingdom."

So Christ is at the gates today. Men, women, and young people, behold your King! Open wide the gates and let Him reign. The Kingdom of God becomes real when we acknowledge its King.

WHAT JESUS SAYS ABOUT LIFE'S DESTINY

... because I live, ye shall live also.

John 14:9

So PERPLEXING AND PAINFUL IS THE SUBJECT OF DEATH THAT many people do not like to think about it. In a recent survey of University students, the question was asked, "If you had a fatal illness, would you desire your doctor to tell you the facts of your condition?" It is interesting to note that over fifty per cent of the students questioned replied, "No, I would not like to know my condition. I would prefer to be kept in ignorance about it." They did not want to face the fact of death.

It is strange that an age which boasts of its enlightenment, glories in its emotional maturity, and is so devoted to objective reality should flee like a little child from this towering event which dominates the whole of life from its beginning. When at last death is faced in the decease of a loved one or friend, it is covered over with sentimentality, buried in flowers, and tucked away behind cemetery walls. We do not want to think about it, and even those familiar with a form of religion may be found evading it.

"What will happen to you after you die?" asked F. B. Meyer of his church warden one day. The man replied, quoting the catechism, "I shall immediately depart into everlasting felicity and bliss," but, he added, "I wish you would not trouble me with such unpleasant subjects." Perhaps it is not so strange that we should shrink away from death. Death—implacable, merciless, relentless—is the last enemy. It comes with measured tread to meet us on the roadway of time, to snatch us out of the land of the living. It defies human plans and purposes. It brings human ambitions to the dust. It shatters human affections. It steals into every home and robs it of loved ones. It breaks eventually, into every life, bringing grief and sorrow. It reaches out its icy hand to stop every living pulse and still the breath of every living thing. Is there an answer anywhere to the problem of death and life's ultimate destiny?

Money cannot buy it off. It slips into the mansions of the rich as easily as it moves into the cottages of the poor. Prestige or power cannot command it. Joseph Stalin, I suppose, was the most powerful political figure of the twentieth century. Literally millions of people were under his absolute control, and yet, before death, he was as helpless as an infant.

Education and human wisdom have no confident answer. Science has no final solution to this problem. It merely affirms that the law of death is as binding as the law of life. No engineer with a slide rule has been able to solve the equation of life and death. No research chemist has run from his laboratory with an exultant shout, "I have the answer to death!" No atomic scientist has been able to apply the power of nuclear physics to the realm of death and blast away the walls of the tomb. Science has mastered the art of mass killing, but it has not learned how to kill death itself. Medicine has wonderfully prolonged life and given it vitality and health, but it, too, must bow before this last relentless enemy.

Sir William Osler, late professor of medicine at Oxford University, speaks for the scientific mind. "Whether across death's threshold we step from life to life or whether we go whence we shall not return, even to the land of darkness, the scientist cannot tell. Nor is this strange. Science is organized knowledge and knowledge is of the things we see. Now the things that are seen are temporal. But of the things that are unseen, science knows nothing and has, at present, no means of knowing anything."

The most brilliant minds often go down into abysmal defeat before the irrationality of death. The contribution of Professor and Madame Curie, the co-discoverers of radium, will be recorded as one of the monumental achievements of this age. On April 19, 1906, Professor Curie was run down by a carriage and instantly killed. The chapter in *The Life of Madame Curie* which describes her wild grief is one of the most tragic and poignant in modern literature. She clung to the body. She kissed the face of the corpse again and again. She wrote in her diary every day to the one who had gone. Among the entries we find these words, "Your coffin was closed and I could see you no more. They came to get you, a sad company. We saw you go down into the deep hole. Then the dreadful procession of people that wanted to take us away. Jack and I resisted. We wanted to see everything to the end. They filled the grave and put flowers on it. Everything is over. Pierre is sleeping in his last sleep beneath the earth. It is the end of everything, everything, everything!" No, science, as such, does not have the answer. The answer must come from the other side, God's side.

We turn to Jesus Christ who alone gives us light on death's darkness. He affirms three tremendous truths about life's destiny. He teaches first that death is not the end of existence. He lifts life out of the flat perspective of three score years and ten and places it in the context of reality. He puts a new dimension to life—infinity. The body will one day be laid aside, but the essential personality will live forever. Jesus saw life penetrating two worlds, the world of man and the world of God; the world of time and the world of eternity. He saw this vividly because He Himself was in both worlds. Human personality, therefore, is of incalculable worth. "For what is a man profited, if he shall gain the whole world, and lose his own soul? . . . (*Mat. 16:26*).

He viewed our existence on earth as probational and preparatory. It was a preparation for that which was larger and greater and for which we were originally fashioned. Beyond this life, He said, there is a higher service to be rendered. "Well done, thou good and faithful servant: thou hast been faithful over a few things, I will make thee ruler over many things: enter thou into the joy of thy lord" (*Mat. 25:21*). On the other side rewards will be received. "Lay up for yourselves treasures in heaven, where neither moth nor rust doth corrupt, and where thieves do not break through nor steal" (*Mat. 6:20*). On the other side there will be fuller fellowship with Himself. He said that He would drink the wine anew with His disciples in the Kingdom ". . . until that day when I drink it new with you in my Father's kingdom" (*Mat. 26:29*). There will be the joy of the Father's House and the glory of the Father's face on the other side.

The Saducees, the rationalists of Jesus' day, rejected the idea of a resurrection. They came to the Master with a question. "Now there were with us seven brethren: and the first, when he had married a wife, deceased, and, having no issue, left his wife unto his brother: Likewise the second also, and the third, unto the seventh. And last of all the woman died also. Therefore in the resurrection whose wife shall she be of the seven? for they all had her.

"Jesus answered and said unto them. Ye do err, not knowing the scriptures, nor the power of God. For in the resurrection they neither marry, nor are given in marriage, but are as the angels of God in heaven. But as touching the resurrection of the dead, have ye not read that which was spoken unto you by God, saying, I am the God of Abraham, and the God of Isaac, and the God of Jacob? God is not the God of the dead, but of the living" (*Mat.* 22:25–32). Yes, He plainly teaches that death is not the end of existence.

Now a second truth—physical death is not the most serious thing that can happen to a person. "Fear not them which kill the body, but are not able to kill the soul: but rather fear him which is able to destroy both soul and body in hell" (*Mat. 10:28*). To be separated from the life of God, to exist on and on, a conscious being apart from the light and the love of the One for whom we are made, is the worst thing that can happen to a person. Even a casual reading of the gospels will make it clear that Jesus came to seek and to save those that are lost, not just for an earthly span of years, but for an eternity.

But supremely Jesus teaches that death has been defeated. The New Testament from beginning to end rings with an exultant note of victory. It is sounded from every believer. Jesus Christ has conquered sin and evil. He has overcome death and the grave. His victory is shared with men. He has invaded the dark domain of death, tracked it down to its lair,

130

gripped it in His nail-pierced hands, and by His life, death, and resurrection, He has subdued its strength, broken its back, and openly displayed His conquest.

No words of the Master assert more boldly His authority over death than those He speaks to Martha at the tomb of her brother, Larzarus. Calmly, with complete confidence, He speaks to the sorrowing sister, "Thy brother shall rise again" (*John 11:23*). She replies, ". . . I know that he shall rise again in the resurrection at the last day" (*John 11:24*). Our Lord then discloses, "I am the resurrection and the life: he that believeth in me, though he were dead, yet shall he live: and whosoever liveth and believeth in me shall never die . . ." (*John 11:25, 26*). Understand what He is saying. I am the life. To know Me, to put your faith in Me, to be in relationship with Me is to share My kind of life which never dies, in which death is simply an incident and not an accident, a doorway and not a decease. Death for the believer is just the beginning. It is not the flickering out of a candle in a dark night. It is the dawning of a new day, the day of God. It is not being imprisoned in the dark walls of a tomb. It is the breaking out of the chrysalis of mortality into a richer, fuller, and more glorious life in God. Death for the Christian is a commencement, a coronation, a consummation of all that life holds and of that purpose which was in the mind of the Heavenly Father for His children before time began. This is the good news of the Risen Lord which Easter proclaims to us. He longs to make it real in our experience.

How may we be sure that His teaching is true? Granted that it is a glorious hope, is there any real ground for believing it? My own conviction is that it is true because Jesus Christ says it is true. I do not know how you feel about Christ, but I have absolute faith in His word. Of all who have ever lived, He supremely merits my confidence. I do not believe that He would lie to me. I cannot conceive of His being deceived on this point. Wherever His teaching touches life, it is true, the truest truth we know. When He touches this tremendous question, I believe we can rest upon His word. In 1867, when Michael Farraday, the famous scientist, was on his deathbed, a friend bent over and asked, "Sir, what are your speculations now?" And Farraday, visibly moved, gathered his ebbing strength and replied, "What are my speculations? I have no speculations, sir. I am resting on a certainty. I know Whom I have believed." The more I know Jesus Christ, the more I am confident that I rest on certainty.

I believe Christ has defeated death because of His own resurrection from the dead. When Tallyrand was struggling for the reconstruction of Europe after the Napoleonic wars, a young man came to him with great enthusiasm and said, "Sir, what Europe needs is a new religion that will be suited for this new day." Tallyrand listened as the young man went on to tell of his ideas. Then he replied. "My young man, if you feel it is the time for a new religion, go out in the highways and byways and begin to elucidate your principles; only be sure that you incorporate them perfectly in your own conduct. Then when you have done that, lay down your life for the people and after you are buried three days, return from the dead and share that victory with your followers. When you have done that, we will be ready to listen to a new religion." Jesus Christ said, "I am the resurrection and the life." On the third day He arose from the dead and verified His authority to speak in terms of victory over death.

The late Dr. Robert E. Speer has this to say about the resurrection. "I believe there is no fact in history better attested than our Lord's Resurrection. It rests upon evidences stronger than any evidence we have of any other event, as strong as the evidence of what took place on July 4th, 1776. I believe we can rest as securely on the evidences of the Resurrection as we can on the evidences that there was a Declaration of Independence. You say, 'But we have the document here and now.' I say, 'We have a living Christ now.' You say, 'Men saw it signed.' I say, 'Men saw Him rise.' You say, 'There is a nation living whose existence testifies to the Declaration of Independence.' I say, 'There is a Kingdom of Christ in existence that bears witness to the fact that something lifted it out of death when He hung on the cross. It was saved by nothing less than His rising again from the dead.' You say, 'The historic evidence does not satisfy everyone.' I say, 'It convinces all who would be convinced if they were to see Him risen with their own eyes.'"

Then I believe Christ has won the victory over death because He demonstrates it in life today. Ever since that first Easter morning when the grief-burdened disciples and followers were encountered by the risen Lord, He has been meeting men and women and sharing His life with them. He does a work in the world today which could not be done by mere memories or hallowed associations. Julius Caesar, for example, is not quickening men into new life today. Martin Luther, great as he was, is not taking men, dead in trespasses and sins, making them clean and giving to them a new life that overcomes evil. But Jesus is doing that. He is taking the drunkard and the profligate, the one in bondage to selfishness and sin, and He is renewing them within, purifying their consciences, and imparting power to be clean and useful in society. He is taking weak people who haven't enough strength of passion to do great wrong, and He is giving them courage to make their lives count for man and God. He is taking good people and making them better, humbling their pride, filling them with a selfless love, giving to them an unshakable hope. He is taking empty and broken lives, aimless and wandering, giving them meaning and significance and sending them out on an eternal mission. He is coming to the lonely and sorrowing with His comfort and companionship, giving them the most precious reality the human heart can desire, that of His Presence.

I recently received a letter from a missionary in Korea. In it he enclosed the greetings of some Korean Christian lepers. "My dear American Christian brothers: We lepers received your kind Christmas presents with deep gratitude. Though outcast and forsaken by our fellowmen because of our incurable disease, we still cherish one bright hope—that through Christ, when relieved from our bodily burden, we shall in pure spirit and body, see our Saviour face to face. Our bodies are cursed and worldly hopes cut off, but we labor for the imperishable, everlasting life that is shining clean and pure through our broken earthenware." Yes, I know Jesus Christ has won the victory over death because He shines clean and pure today in the broken earthenware of the lives of His followers.

I know this because He verifies it in the personal experience of His followers. Thomas, the disciple, stoutly refused to believe what others told him about Christ's resurrection from the dead. ". . . But he said unto them, Except I shall see in his hands the print of the nails, and put my finger into the print of the nails, and thrust my hand into his side, I will not believe"

(*John 20:25*). I have to have evidence. Jesus did not deny him nor rebuke him. He appeared to him and said, "Reach hither thy finger, and behold my hands; and reach hither thy hand, and thrust it into my side: and be not faithless, but believing" (*John 20:27*).

I believe that Jesus Christ will manifest His living presence to anyone who really wants to know Him, anyone who is really willing to walk His way of life and acknowledge Him to be the true Lord. Hudson Taylor once said, "No one can talk aloud to Jesus Christ for five minutes, desiring to know Him and to do His will without having something happen." Jesus Christ will verify Himself.

A well-known journalist tells of listening to a Russian lecturer in Moscow who attacked the Christian faith for ninety minutes and proved to his own satisfaction, at least, that faith in God was a dying survival of Capitalism. When he finished, he invited discussion. A young village priest stepped forward and asked permission to speak. "Not more than five minutes," the speaker replied. "I shall not be so long," replied the priest. He ascended the platform and addressed the audience. "Brothers and sisters, Christ is risen!" As one man, the audience replied, "He is risen indeed!"—the familiar response of Russian believers. "I have finished," said the priest. "I have nothing more to say."

To the problem of death and life's destiny we say, "Jesus Christ is risen." Nothing more need be said.

WHAT JESUS SAYS ABOUT TRUE FAITH

He that hath the Son hath life; and he that hath not the Son of God hath not life.

I John 5:12

WHO IS THE TRUE CHRISTIAN? IT IS ASTONISHING TO DISCOVER how much confusion there is on this subject, even among people who have been reared in the atmosphere of the Christian church. Some are very broad and very generous in their definition. A true Christian to them is anyone who is living in the general traditions of society—one, let us say, who cooks his food and does not tear it raw from the bone; one who wears clothes according to the accepted custom, and who has only one wife at a time. But opinions appear to be broadening. The term "Christian" is often loosely applied to anyone who has the veneer and polish of our modern western civilization, regardless of the condition of the heart or personal relationship to the living God.

On the other hand, others are not so liberal in their classification. They feel that a true Christian is a very rare, saintly individual. To make the grade, he must be a paragon of flaw-

less virtue with an angelic disposition. He must live some-
where far from ordinary behavior, suspended between
heaven and earth, unrelated to realistic living and unsuited
for the workaday world we know. These individuals insist that
". . . many are called, but few chosen." As the little boy returning from Sunday School said: "Mother, today they talked
about cold Christians." "Cold Christians!" the mother ex-
claimed. "What did they say?" "Well," replied the boy, "they
talked on the verse 'many are cold and a few are frozen!' " In
this view Christianity is limited to just a very, very few—to "me
and thee, and I am not so sure of thee!"

Who is right? Where does the truth lie and how may we define genuine Christianity? Some may feel that they are true
Christians when, really, they are not. Others may fear they
are not when, really, they are. So we turn to the Bible and
particularly to the New Testament for our definition of the
nature of a true Christian. I think the simplest and in many
ways the most profound definition is given in I John 5:12: "He
that hath the Son (Christ) hath life; and he that hath not the
Son of God hath not life." Thus Christianity is described in
terms of life. It is described as a living relationship with the
source of life, Jesus Christ. I like to define it this way: "Christianity is the life of God in the soul of man through personal
trust in Jesus Christ as Saviour and Lord." In order to make
this truth clear, let us consider it first in the negative—what a
Christian is not; and thus sharpening our understanding, let
us turn later to the positive truth of the subject.

A true Christian is not merely a decent fellow who is kind
and good, who is substantial and sober, who is a solid citizen
and a good husband and father. Christ certainly ought to make
a man like that, but this is not the heart or the substance of

137

Christianity. Rather, these virtues are the fruit of Christianity. The true Christian is not merely a church member who has been baptized, catechized, and processed through an ecclesiastical organization. Often, we consider Christianity as a process. We think of it somewhat like an orange, picked, washed, wrapped, packed, and then shipped up to the Pearly Gates, regardless of the condition of the fruit. But this is not Christianity. There is no such routine process, no mechanical procedure whereby an individual may be wrapped, packaged, and delivered above by a church, apart from a personal relationship with God.

Judas Iscariot, I suppose would have passed the membership committee of almost any church. He was to all outward appearances sincere. He made an affirmation of faith. He observed religious services. But to attend services, to give generously to a cause, and to put one's hand to work, laudable as these things may be, is not the essence of Christianity. It is rather the outcome of a relationship and a life. Of course, the true Christian will seek the church and its causes, the way a child seeks a father and the father's house. But seeking the church does not establish in itself this relationship with the living God.

A true Christian is not merely one who does not do things. Strangely enough, there is a point of view that persists in thinking, "The more things I do not do, the more truly a Christian I am. I do not lie, or cheat, or steal. I do not swear or drink. I do not carouse. I do not do this; I do not do that. Therefore, I am a Christian." No accumulation of negatives can ever bring man into the positive life of Christ. A house cannot be built out of rejected material. The gospel is "good news," "glad tidings," and certainly it is not glad tidings to be told that salvation is found by barricading oneself from life and loading oneself with all kinds of restrictions. The early Christians were out in the streets and thoroughfares singing their joy. They had been delivered. They had entered into a new life and were in the fellowship of God. It was positive. It broke the patterns of the old by the power of a new impulse. It was not barricading life and barring it from certain evils. It was setting life free.

Let it be said also that a Christian is not merely one who affirms a doctrinal belief. One may subscribe to all the points of the catechism and still not be a true Christian. The Bible says," . . . the devils also believe, and tremble" (*James 2:19*). In fact, the most orthodox statements about Jesus in the days of His flesh were from people possessed with demons. Whenever they were confronted by Jesus of Nazareth, they cried out and said, "What have we to do with thee, Jesus, thou Son of God?" Long before the disciples had come to that position of faith, the demons were crying it. They believed all right, but their belief was not the kind that submitted to the authority of Christ or entrusted their lives to Him. Christianity is more than believing certain doctrines. It is good to believe truth. Truth is absolutely essential to the knowledge of God, but truth may be used somewhat like the rails on a railroad track; they are necessary to keep the train going in the right direction, but the rails in themselves do not provide the power nor move the passengers. Doctrine and the truths of Christ in the Bible are there to keep us on the way of life with God, but in themselves they are not life-giving.

Finally, a Christian is not one who is doing the best he can, trying to work his way or pay his way to God. So many times people have said to me, "Well, I'm doing the best I can." I commend their sincerity, but to do the best you can and to live up to what light you have is not Christianity.

One summer during a college vacation, I shipped out as a deck hand on one of the old Matson liners. I was not long on that cruise when I discovered that there were three categories of people on board. There was the crew, from the captain down to me—and that was very far down! We were working our way. We were there because we had a job to do. We could not have stayed on board if we had ceased to work. There was another class, the passengers. They were not working. They were enjoying themselves on the cruise, sunning themselves in deck chairs, enjoying the good food in the dining room, walking the decks. They were there because they had paid their way. They had bought passage on that ship and for that reason had the right to enjoy all its privileges. But there was still another class; the children of the passengers. They were not working, neither did they pay their way, but they were welcomed nevertheless. In fact, they had the best time of all, clambering and playing all over the ship. They were there because of a relationship. They were the children of parents who had paid for them and were taking them along with them on the voyage.

On this cruise with God into real salvation and life, there is only one class on board. No one can get on the ship because he pays his way. He is on board only because he is in relationship to the One who runs and operates the vessel. He is there only because he is a child of God through Jesus Christ. "Not by works of righteousness which we have done," writes the Apostle in Titus 3:5, "but according to his mercy he has saved us. . . ." Or again in Ephesians 2:8, "By grace are ye saved through faith; and that not of yourselves: it is the gift of God: Not of your works, lest any man should boast." We take our position in Christ because of His work for us—His righteousness, His merit, His redeeming power, His grace, His marvelous gift of salvation. It is not through our sacrifice, but through His sacrifice; not through our efforts, but through His efforts; not through what we are, but through what He is. Eternal life is given to us freely and accepted by a simple act of faith.

What would I do without my physical existence? Yet, I did not earn it or work for it. It was given to me. Of course, I recognize with gratitude those who gave my life to me, and I want to respond to them in love. But I cannot earn it, I cannot work for it, or pay for it.

Love, also, may only be received one way: as a gift. You can't buy love. You can't make a contract for love to be delivered on the basis of certain demands. Love is graciously, freely offered. Anything less than that ceases to be real love. You may respond to it and seek to be worthy of it, but real love comes as a free gift of the heart. In the same manner, we enter into a relationship with the living God in Christ Jesus by a believing, grateful response to what He has already done for us.

> It is not thy repentance, sorrow or tears
> That brings to thee salvation
> Or drives away thy fears.
> It is the cross of Jesus,
> The death He there did die
> That wrought out full salvation
> For such as you and I.
> It is not what thou doest,

Or what is left undone,
Or giving up a habit,
By which salvation's won.

James H. Gray

Now let's turn to the positive aspect of who is the true Christian. What are the characteristics of the real child of God? I think, first of all, that a true Christian is one who agrees with Christ. Certainly we must begin here. Our Lord had many things to say about the meaning of life, about the Heavenly Father, and relationships between man and God. We accept Christ's Word as final. We believe Him to be the supreme teacher and authority on matters of faith and life. We agree with Jesus Christ. This agreement is at the heart of Christianity. When Jesus Christ tells us that man needs a Saviour, that he has lost his way and needs a shepherd to find him and restore him, that the heart of man is evil and needs forgiveness, that all the strivings of man cannot attain to God, but man must needs be lifted there on the arms of grace, then we believe what Jesus says. We start here. In this day of confusion, with humanity battered and blasted with two ruinous wars, and in this hour of bitter disillusionment and anxiety, people still cling to their self-sufficiency. It is hard for a man to admit that by his own strength and wisdom he cannot find God. For him to submit himself as a recipient, rather than a builder of salvation by his own efforts, is not easy. But here we must begin. A true Christian starts with the understanding that he cannot save himself, that he needs One to save him. He turns to Jesus Christ as the answer to his need.

There are many things that prompt us to turn to Jesus Christ like this. It may be the search for reality, a deep hunger

142

to know the truth. We may be driven by a dissatisfaction with the transitory and the changing aspects of man's knowledge, a longing for that which is solid and sure and steadfast, a desire to ground the soul upon eternal things that will abide and never pass away. In this mood, many have turned to Christ and found Him to be the Way, the Truth, and the Life.

Another may have a desire for fellowship, an inner loneliness that recognizes that all the human companionship in the world will not answer the cry of the heart for fellowship with God. Seeking that kind of a relationship, he turns to Christ, who gives it.

Yet another is prompted to consider Christ out of a quest for certainty about eternal things. In this sophisticated day, a good many people pride themselves that they are not "otherworldly," dismissing the eternal aspect of existence and considering only today. But I have seen enough people in time of sorrow and counseled enough of the so-called "self-sufficient" to know that at the graveside there is always a wistfulness to know a life that will never end. Love continues after separation and asks profound questions: "Where is my loved one?" "Will we be together again? Does life simply go out like a flickering candle, extinguished in a gust of wind to leave nothing but darkness?" So the quest for things that will abide, and certainty about tomorrow has brought many to Him who said, "I am the resurrection, and the life: he that believeth in me, though he were dead, yet shall he live: whosoever liveth and believeth in me shall never die . . ." (*John 11:25, 26*). They have found in Christ Jesus a positive knowledge of eternal things.

I think some people recognize the need for direction in life. There are so many conflicting drives that if we are not careful, we become subject to frustration and futility. They ask, "What does it all add up to? What am I doing with my life? Am I really getting anywhere or doing anything that really counts?"

It was this that first caused me to seek God. I could not find the formula for life, why I was here, what was really important, what gave value and meaning to existence. The key was eluding my grasp. Life was losing its significance, its flavor and zest. I thought, "Certainly if there is within me the desire to live a meaningful life and if there is a Creator in the universe, He must have an answer!" I turned to Him who has said, ". . . he that followeth me shall not walk in darkness, but shall have the light of life." I found He makes good these words.

Our basic need is for forgiveness and peace with God. To be convinced that there is a God and to suspect that He is holy, righteous, and just, throws into contrast the opposite condition that we know in our own lives. To face realistically our jealousies, our hypocrisies, our inconsistencies, our evil thoughts, our unforgiving attitudes—really to see the kind of people we are—is to be convinced of a fundamental need which no one of us in ourselves can meet. The point of reconciliation between us and the living God of Truth is His forgiveness.

David was a good man, a man after God's own heart. But there came a day when David realized that he had one urgent, pressing need. ". . . my sin," he said, "is ever before me." He needed forgiveness.

Peter was willing to forsake all and follow Christ. He was ready to do much for the Master, yet there came a time after his denial of Christ when he flung himself, weeping, out into the darkness. Then Peter knew he had one fundamental need. He needed forgiveness and restoration to fellowship with Jesus Christ.

Saul of Tarsus was brilliant and well educated. He felt secure in his self-righteousness and his work of religion, until he was confronted by the truth and holiness of the risen Lord. Then he knew that all his religiousness and righteousness were as nothing. He needed forgiveness and he needed to be reconciled to his God.

William Wilberforce was one of the guiding spirits of the Reform Movement in England during the nineteenth century. This youth, hunchbacked and deformed physically, was gifted with a brilliant mind and a very gracious, winsome personality. By the time he was in his early twenties, he had become the close companion of the younger Pitt. These two men were destined to go far in the service of their country and to have great influence among men. One summer, as they were traveling on the Continent together, Wilberforce had in his bag a copy of Doddridge's book, *The Rise and Progress of the Soul,* a very penetrating analysis of the human heart and its need. While reading that book, he became aware of his need of divine forgiveness. It was as though an arrow pierced his heart. He had always believed there was a God, but now he saw the *holiness* of God, and against it the black stain of his sinful heart. In the white light of living truth, he realized that unless he was a forgiven man, he was a lost man. He wrote in his diary of his anguish, "Oh, God, my sin! My sin! My awful sin! Roll the burden of it from my heart." There was but one place to go with his burdened soul—to the cross of Calvary and the sinner's Friend. Before long he found in Christ the matchless grace of God, forgiveness and a new life—a new life which was used to uplift humanity as few lives have ever been used.

These are some of the many impulses that bring us to Jesus Christ. Essentially, they come back to the recognition that we have certain basic needs that we cannot satisfy but that Christ can. In this we agree with Christ. We also agree that the purpose of our living is to do the will of God.

A true Christian not only agrees with Christ but believes in Him; that is, he has an essential confidence that Jesus Christ is who He Himself says He is and that He will do what He promises to do. "As many as received him, to them gave he power to become the sons of God, even to them that believe on his name" (*John 1:12*). His name represents His character and the nature of His person. To trust Jesus Christ with your very soul is vital to being a real Christian.

This does not necessitate knowing all the truths about Christ or believing them all. It does not mean that we have to know the Bible from cover to cover or to consent to all that is contained in the creeds of the church. It is not faith in a theology that saves us. It is not faith in a creed that redeems us. It is personal confidence and commitment to Jesus Christ Himself.

The bride, for example, may not know all about the young man she has chosen to be her husband. She will learn many things about him in the years to come. But she knows about him and believes in him enough to give herself to him. So, real faith in Jesus Christ is to know enough about Him and to have enough confidence in Him to entrust yourself to Him. The heart of Christian belief is very simple. It is personal—I believe that in His great love the Son of God dwelt among men to show me the way, to reveal the Father's will, and to lead me home. I believe that Christ died for me, that He took my place and suffered for my sins, that He is my Saviour. I believe that Christ lives for me, that He was victorious over sin, death, and hell, and now He sits at the right hand of the Father, my all-sufficient Lord. He is my Guide, my Friend, my Redeemer. I trust myself to Him. I respond by committing my life to Him.

John G. Paton of the New Hebrides was translating the Gospel of St. John into an aboriginal language. In his translation he came to the twelfth verse in the first chapter: "As many as received him, to them gave he power to become the sons of God, even to them that believe on his name. . . ." He could not find the native word for "belief" or "trust." He inquired here and there as he went about and listened attentively for clues. No such word came to his attention. One day, as he was working at his desk, a native boy entered on an errand and stood respectfully by the missionary's desk. Mr. Paton, occupied for the moment and seeing the boy standing there, pointed to a chair and said, "Sit down." Now a chair was a rather new object to this boy who was used to sitting on the floor. It was a common wicker chair, but he had had no experience with such an article of furniture. He looked at it suspiciously for a moment and asked the missionary what he meant. He replied, "Sit down in it and rest yourself!" The boy carefully walked over to the seat and very gingerly eased himself down into it, waited a moment, and then relaxed with an expression of relief. "Well," he said, "I can trust this chair, it will hold me up!" "Say that word again," said the missionary excitedly, "It is the very one I've been looking for." He was right. To trust Christ means to put your weight upon Him, to let Him hold you up. You can walk around and around a chair, analyzing it, investigating it, hearing lectures on it, discussing it, but it will do you no good until you sit on it, and relax. We are not only to consider Christ; we are to put our weight on Him and trust Him.

Recently, I took a flight in a new type plane. I had never been in this particular type of plane before. I had read something of it; I liked its looks, and had to take it to meet an engagement. So I got on board and it took me safely there. Suppose that I had had some doubts or reservations about the plane. I could have read volumes on the theory of aerodynamics and studied the structure of the plane. I could have checked all the instruments on the panel. They might have allowed me to walk out on the wings and to test the fuselage to see that it was sound. I could have listened to the motors as they were being tuned up. By these means and others, I might have been convinced beyond a doubt that the plane was reliable and would take me where I wanted to go. But if I did not get on board, it would have done me no good.

Often, we wait to further investigate this matter of Christ and Christianity. We hear arguments for Him. We listen to testimony of what He has done for others. We come to the point where we say, "Certainly, I am convinced in my mind that Jesus Christ is Lord and Saviour." But that is not enough. There must be an act of commitment that gets the whole life on board and trusts Him to do for us what He has said He would do. This is the kind of faith that unites us to Christ.

Our text emphasizes the action aspect of faith. "As *many as received him,* to them gave he power to become the sons of God. . . ." To receive may be understood as "to reach out and take," or "to appropriate." The faith that unites us to the Saviour is a positive, intelligent understanding faith, an ap-

148

propriation of Jesus Christ. He has made certain promises and provisions. He has demonstrated His sincerity by giving His life for us on the cross. He has demonstrated His faithfulness in thousands of lives. He has given us His inviolate word in the Scriptures. The moment we take Him seriously and believe that He will do for us what He said He would do, in that moment we are true Christians.

Let us return to the illustration of the bride and groom. Their desire to be united in marriage is the result of some knowledge of each other and a mutual attraction. But still more is needed to be married. They need to stand before the altar and solemnly give themselves to one another. It is this covenant of confidence, this self-giving and receiving, this contract grounded upon the other's sincerity and backed by the sharing of all of life that is at the heart of the marriage ceremony. Marriage is not based upon feelings and emotion, though these may attend it. It is not determined by ability, experience, or will power. Marriage is valid the moment two people give themselves to one another forever.

In the same way, the soul is united to Jesus Christ. He has given Himself to us in infinite love through His life, death, and resurrection. He has spoken to us an everlasting "Yes." The moment we respond to Him, yield Him our hearts, and trust Him, we are His forever.

WHAT JESUS SAYS ABOUT MANAGING
OUR UNMANAGEABLES

There is nothing from without a man, that entering into him can defile him: but the things which come out of him, those are they that defile the man.

Mark 7:15

WE ARE TREMENDOUSLY CONCERNED THESE DAYS TO FIND A WAY to manage a wild and savage world. The beast of war roars in his fragile cage, reaching out a vicious paw to maul the passerby and send frightened keepers scurrying to find stronger bolts and bars lest atomic destruction break out from restraint. There is only one matter of greater concern to many, and that is how to manage ourselves—how to control the wild and willful world within us.

Dr. Alfred E. Luccock calls attention to an Associated Press dispatch of about a year ago which stated that a certain Mr. Solomon A. Stephen had died at the age of one hundred. The principle feature of the story was not the length of his life, but the fact that for sixty-seven years, Mr. Stephen had been manager of the zoo at Cincinnati, Ohio. He had come to that

150

city from New York in 1875 to deliver an elephant, and had
remained to look after it and the other animals. All of us spend
a great deal of time managing a zoo, often without noticeable
success—I mean the zoo inside us.

I was introduced to the world of zoo life by our children,
who at an early age decided it was time for their parents to be
informed about the facts of animal existence. They escorted
us to the zoo so often that I became personally acquainted
with every parrot and pachyderm in the place. There are
beautiful animals in the zoo—deer, zebra, elk, and birds of
brilliant plumage. Odd animals are there too—the giraffe, the
kangaroo, and assorted varieties of monkeys. Then there are
carniverous beasts, the tiger, the lion, the grizzly bear, well
secured behind parapet and bars.

Some years ago, a Chicago newspaper carried on an inten-
sive campaign with the local zoo. The editor declared, "The
children of our city know every rare and exotic animal from
the remotest places of earth, but many of them have never
seen a sheep or looked into the gentle eyes of a cow. Please
kind sir, could we not place a cow in the zoo and show our
children that milk does not originate in a bottling machine?"

And I have discovered that other zoo—the zoo within myself, filled with all kinds of weird creatures, many of them
quite undomesticated, wild and most difficult to handle. Nor
do I think I am unique in this. Carl Sandburg in his poem
Wilderness writes, "There is a wolf in me." There are other
animals of evil to be fought and tamed. Who has not had the
lion of temper rage and roar from within? Who has not heard
the restless footfall of the tiger of envy pacing up and down
the pens of the soul? Who has not caught his jealous snarl?
Who has not found within a loathsome jackal of criticism,

feeding on the carrion of human failure, and biting and tearing at people better than ourselves? Who has not recoiled at the lying serpent of deceit slithering through life and gliding across the tongue?

Barnyard animals are there, too. The peacock of pride struts up and down, preening his plumage. The braying mule of stubbornness that will not be moved, the old swine grunting in the mud and shoving others aside—they are all there.

Robert Browning, looking at the portrait of one of the richest industrial figures of his time, said, "He looks like a retired panther." The man's fierce competitive days of strangling his rivals were over, and he had assumed a look of benevolent kindliness. In me, the old panther never seems to retire but keeps bounding out, just when I think I have him safely pensioned off. I find I need help. I cannot manage the zoo within me. I wonder how you are doing with your zoo—the inner desires and disposition, the selfishness and the sin?

Turning to the Bible, I find some very practical and sound advice on how to handle the heart and manage life's unmanageables. The Bible suggests that we begin by recognizing the animals within and calling them by their right names. "If we confess our sins, he is faithful and just to forgive us our sins, and to cleanse us from all unrighteousness" (*I John 1:9*).

Beside every cage in the zoo there is a little sign giving both the Latin and the English name of the animal. Part of the zoo-keeper's job is to make sure that every animal is properly designated and rightly placed. Imagine the confusion and the danger if he did not arrange the animals correctly. He might put the lion in with the lamb or allow children to pet the tiger.

People have long quarreled with the names the Bible gives

to the issues of the heart. Many violently disagree with the Christian diagnosis of human nature. They take strong issue with what Jesus has to say about the wild things within. Nevertheless, the Word of God clearly teaches that there are wild and savage things in the soul and He calls them sin. "The heart is deceitful above all things, and desperately wicked . . ." (*Jer. 17:9*).

The twentieth century dawned in rosy optimism about man. There is nothing really bad in us, we were told. These snarling moods and wrong motives are just repressions; feed them, give them room, stop calling them such bad names and they will behave themselves. We were almost convinced. Then two terrible world wars broke in fury upon us, leaving humanity maimed and mangled. If we would not face the sin within us, we were compelled to confront it in the world around us. We have taken another look at human nature, and we are sobered.

Thomas Beecher, the venerable old preacher, was a great lover of truth. He could not tolerate deceit in any form. Yet, he had in his church a clock which was always too fast or too slow. One day, in desperation, he put a sign over the clock: "Don't blame my hands; the trouble lies deeper." The trouble with humanity lies deeper than circumstances. It lies in the soul, within us.

The press recently carried the announcement of the death of the famous English philosopher, Dr. C. E. M. Joad of the University of London. For years he was a vociferous agnostic and opponent of Christianity. He loved to say, "When the mind becomes old and begins to decay, it becomes matted with God-webs." But as the second World War progressed and became more terrible, he began to doubt that evil was something that could be cured by socialism, sociology, and psycho-analysis. He considered again what the gospel of Christ had to say and he began to believe. He said, "When war came, the existence of evil hit me in the face. I see now that evil is en-demic in man and that the Christian doctrine of original sin expresses a deep and essential insight into human nature." Of his rediscovered faith he says, "It affords me light to live by in an ever-darkening world."

One of the fundamental fallacies of Marxism is that it will not label correctly the wild things of the human heart. It be-lieves that changed circumstances will change human nature. Marxism does not go deep enough, and hence it is doomed to frustration; it will never arrive. It is tragic that we do not take the word of Jesus seriously when He says to us in Mark 7:15, "There is nothing from without a man, that entering into him can defile him. . . ." That is, circumstances and things around him do not cause the trouble ". . . but the things which come out of him, those are they that defile the man." . . . "For from within, out of the heart of men, proceed evil thoughts, adul-teries, fornications, murders, thefts, covetousness, wickedness, deceit, lasciviousness, an evil eye, blasphemy, pride, foolish-ness: All these evil things come from within and defile the man" (*Mark 7:21–23*).

Let me begin, then, to manage my unmanageables by call-ing them by their right names. Let me not evade them. Let me not excuse myself, but in the clear light of God let me say, "These things are evil. They spring from my sinful heart." To confess means "to say with." Let me then agree with God's diagnosis and description of my trouble. We start here.

Next, keep the dangerous animals locked behind bars. I am sure that few of us would enjoy a zoo if we knew that some of the lions and tigers were loose. The grounds would quickly empty of people. The roar of the lion in the lion house is rather entertaining, but if you are camping alone on the African veldt, the same sound arouses different sensations. Yet in recent years a very strange code of conduct has been advocated. It says, express yourselves. Let your animal appetites loose. If you know lust, indulge it. If you are angry, go ahead, blow your top! If you don't like social convention, throw it aside. Be yourself, even if it is your worst self. When this happens, the animals run the zoo and the keepers get behind the bars. The law of the jungle takes over. No wonder there are so many confused and chaotic lives, so much unhappiness in our homes, and so much emptiness in our hearts. No wonder young people flounder in conflict of desire and frustration.

Mr. Ted De Grazia, an artist in Tucson, Arizona, has circulated a little advertisement of his studio which says: "A great work of art invites you to renounce the world and embrace yourself, not out of goodness, but because the least impulse or appetite within you may be of greater real consequence than all the weight and import of the world's affairs." There is in De Grazia's paintings the suggestion that if the onlooker will only search out and gratify the hidden wickednesses, the secret lusts that are in him, then that search and that gratification may be of more real importance to man's salvation than all the noble pronouncements and good intentions in the world.

There are few people who are as crude in expressing their philosophy, but I would remind you that it is a current attitude widely held. Express yourself. But you cannot let the wild things loose in your life without experiencing the destruction of all that is high and holy. "For the wages of sin is death . . ." (*Rom. 6:23*).

Time magazine for August 1952, carried the story of a California lady snake tamer. The article entitled "Creeping Death" states, "Of all her snakes, sixty-four-year-old Grace Wiley loved the cobra best. He was the most intelligent and most easily tamed. 'It is just that people are afraid to tame cobras,' she said. Grace Wiley had never been afraid. She loved reptiles and handled them patiently and lovingly. She filled her home in Cypress, California with over a hundred of them— King and Queen, the cobras; Roxie, the nine-foot python; Perky, the water moccasin. One day she agreed to pose for a picture with her newest pet, a five-foot cobra just received from India. To get the cobra ready for the picture she patted its head, stroked its back, quietly coaxed it to extend its hood and as the cobra's head bobbed back and forth rhythmically, Mrs. Wiley began to fear that it was not responding well. 'It's getting nervous' she said. 'I had better put it away.' And as she reached for it, the cobra struck. For a full thirty seconds she struggled to get the needle-point fangs out of her middle finger, pressing with all her strength against the cobra's locked jaws. When she had torn the snake loose, she returned it to its cage and calmly instructed the photographer to apply the tourniquet to her wrist and elbow. She told him where to find needles and stimulants. But the needles were rusty and the vials broke in the photographer's hands. 'Take me to the hospital at once,' she said. 'This is serious.' But all the aid at the Long Beach Hospital was of no avail to save this woman. Her throat muscles contracted and she became paralyzed. Just exactly one hour and forty minutes after she had been bitten, her body suddenly stiffened and she lay dead on the hospital bed."

You cannot take a lie into your life and fondle it without being bitten. You cannot indulge lust and not have it poison love and destroy decency. You cannot let greed and bitterness twine about your heart and not be hurt. You cannot let selfishness or pride crawl into your life without having them bury their fangs in you. Sin is deadly. The Bible states this very clearly. ". . . the wages of sin is death." We endeavor to call it by a different name, but its nature remains. ". . . the soul that sinneth it shall die," because sin does violence to the will of God and sin destroys the life of man.

The first word that Jesus had to say in His public ministry was, *"Repent!"* Change your attitude! Change your behavior concerning evil. Break with it. Lock it up and put it away. Repent! Man is not made to live like a beast; he is meant to live in fellowship with a Holy God and walk as His son in the world.

In managing your zoo, feed the good animals. A visitor to the Southern Mountains was chatting with an old mountaineer who had two dogs about the same size. The dogs were fighting continually. The visitor asked the mountaineer which dog usually won. The man chewed his tobacco for awhile in silence and then he said, "The one I feeds the most!"

Within the believer there are two natures steadily at war; the new nature, by the Spirit of God, endeavoring to make love, truth, purity, humility, and godliness supreme, and the old nature, fighting to place self, darkness, and evil on top. The one that is fed the most is the one that wins. Feed your lower nature by suggestive reading, by tawdry films or T.V. shows, by careless conversation, by loose associations and what happens? It is on top. But feed your higher nature, the things of God and goodness, and the higher nature will be on top.

Let us then nourish the mind with the Word of God. ". . . Man shall not live by bread alone, but by every word that proceedeth out of the mouth of God" (*Mat. 4:4*). The Bible is food for man's spiritual nature. "Blessed is the man that walketh not in the counsel of the ungodly, nor standeth in the way of sinners, not sitteth in the seat of the scornful. But his delight is in the law of the Lord; and in his law doth he meditate day and night. And he shall be like a tree planted by the rivers of water, . . . his leaf also shall not wither; and whatsoever he doeth shall prosper" (*Psa. 1:1–3*). Let me put into my mind the truths of the Word of God, meditate on them day and night, feed the spiritual life with a knowledge of God and His will in Christ, and it will grow in strength.

The Chinese Communists, with diabolical cleverness, have developed a technique called "brain washing" to remove the last vestige of "capitalist" or "imperialist" thought from the mind of a suspect. It is not a very complicated process. They simply take the individual and subject him to a steady barrage of indoctrination. They question him. They contradict his answers. They hammer home half-truths, distortions, falsehoods. The principles and dogmas of the party line are ceaselessly sounded, until over a period of time the plastic material of the mind is molded to their pattern. When one is subjected to this process without respite, there often comes a breaking point, a counter-conversion, and one who once hated communism becomes a fanatical follower of Marx.

It is a terrible business! Yet in America today, our minds are being subjected in a real way to "brain washing." It's going on all the time, not deliberately or consciously but, nevertheless, truly. It comes over the television sets, through the magazines and periodicals, in the pattern of secular life around us. And if we are not careful, our minds will be just as truly shaped in the materialism and godlessness of American thought as that of the Communist by "brain washing." Rather, let us put into our minds the clear truth of God and His Word—meditating, assimilating, responding, orienting ourselves to God and His purposes and provisions in Jesus Christ.

Jesus said, "Abide in me, and I in you. As the branch cannot bear fruit of itself, except it abide in the vine; no more can ye, except ye abide in me. I am the vine, ye are the branches: He that abideth in me, and I in him, the same bringeth forth much fruit: for without me ye can do nothing" (*John 15:4, 5*).

That is, continue in this fellowship of truth with me. Paul said, ". . . be not conformed to this world: but be ye transformed by the renewing of your mind, that ye may prove what is that good, and acceptable, and perfect, will of God" (*Rom. 12:2*). To overcome the effect of non-Christian ideas, let me come to the Bible day by day, prayerfully, humbly, and with real purpose. Let me learn what God wants to say to me, then put it into action.

When our Lord was tempted in the wilderness, three times He answered the Adversary with a quotation, "Thus saith the Lord." He mastered evil through an intimate knowledge of God's Word which He had in His heart. No man can master evil in life until he lets the Word of God feed him. This is not a theory any more than "brain washing" is a theory. It is real.

We overcome in the Word of truth—the Bible, known, trusted, obeyed.

Let us feed our hearts with Christian fellowship. God has made us to dwell in families in Christ and we need fellowship with other Christians. I believe the hour of worship on the Lord's Day is essential, but we must go beyond that to smaller groups where we share the wonderful things of our Lord and catch from each other the inspiration of godly living. In homes, in small fellowship prayer groups, or in conferences—wherever we are together with Christ at the center we sense our oneness in Him and our hearts are fed.

At any time or place we may feed our souls on Christ. Brother Lawrence, among the pots and pans of the monastery, had such a radiant spirit and godly life that people came from afar to learn the ways of the Lord. He had wanted to be a learned scholar, but that was denied him. He had dreamed of a ministry before the altar but found himself in a kitchen. At first he was discouraged. Then he remembered, "God is here, right here in the kitchen. Let me recognize Him." He practiced the presence of God, and it transformed his life and brought the hungry hearted from afar to learn of Christ in a kitchen.

To manage the wild things within us, we also need a strong Keeper. During my college days, there was a boy whose room down the hall from me was a continual mess. When one's room is branded "messy" by college students, it's *really* messy. One evening we were endeavoring to crowd into his room, and he said somewhat apologetically, "What I need is a little system." "Oh, no," said one of the boys, "you need a little wife to help you take care of these matters."

Personal endeavor and discipline is essential, but there comes a time when life is more than we can master by ourselves. We need a Keeper for the heart. Jesus Christ came to handle the problem of sin and to help us manage our unmanageables. For this purpose He became incarnate and took upon Himself our nature. He lived with us and identified Himself with our needs. He tracked sin down to its lair and uncovered its deadly coils. On Calvary He met the full fury of evil's assault and conquered it by His resurrection. Now He shares His victory with us and He will impart His purity and power to every trusting, yielded life.

Paul writes, "This is a faithful saying, and worthy of all acceptation, that Christ Jesus came into the world to save sinners; of whom I am chief." He came to save us not only from sin's penalty, but from sin's power. And if we can take it to Christ, call it by its true name, confess it, turn from it, and surrender it to Him, we can rely upon His grace and power to handle that wrong thing in our life.

The demoniac of Gadara roamed naked and unmanageable among the tombs; no one could bind him. He cried continually, cutting himself with stones, possessed of foul spirits. Then Jesus came. With a word He cast the foul things out of the demoniac's life. The man was found seated at the feet of Jesus, clothed and in his right mind.

The poor paralytic in a helpless condition was lowered through the tiles of the roof by his friends and placed before our Lord. Jesus said to him, "Son, be of good cheer, thy sins are forgiven thee. Arise, take up thy bed and walk." And he arose free.

Zaccheus, whose soul was imprisoned with greed for gold, had an interview with Jesus. When he came from that luncheon engagement he said, "Behold, the half of my goods I give to the poor and if I have wronged any man, I restore to him fourfold." The wrong things were righted in his life.

When the sinful woman wept at Jesus' feet, bathing them with her tears and wiping them with her tresses, our Lord said to her, "Thy sins be forgiven thee." He had put pure love in her life. Jesus can do this. Make Him the Keeper of your life.

There would be no problem in the zoo at all, if the nature of all the wild animals was transformed. The Prophet Jeremiah raised the rhetorical question, "Can . . . the leopard change his spots? then may ye also do good, that are accustomed to do evil?" (*Jer. 13:23*). Can the leopard change his spots? No. But God can, and here is the miracle of His grace and power. He can make our weak points places of strength. "Therefore if any man be in Christ, he is a new creature: old things are passed away; behold, all things are become new" (*II Cor. 5:17*). Listen to this. "Know ye not that the unrighteous shall not inherit the kingdom of God? Be not deceived: neither fornicators, nor idolaters, nor adulterers, nor effeminate, nor abusers of themselves with mankind, nor thieves, nor covetous, nor drunkards, nor revilers, nor extortioners, shall inherit the kingdom of God. And such were some of you: but ye are washed, but ye are sanctified, but ye are justified in the name of the Lord Jesus, and by the Spirit of our God" (*I Cor. 6:9–11*). After all, this is the final solution to the problem, changing the nature of the heart, giving new drives and disposition. Christ is not satisfied with keeping bad things in check. He purposes to make bad things good, to take the very areas of our failure and make them places of moral power.

First then, let us face our sins in confession. Second, repent of the sin in our lives. Third, surrender ourselves to Christ and His will. There is a last step. Make the wrong right with others.

Is temper your trouble? The next time you injure someone through your expression of temper, go to that individual and humbly say, "I'm sorry that I hurt you with my temper. Forgive me, for Christ's sake." If you do that, I guarantee that quicker than you believe possible, your temper will be tamed.

Are criticism and gossip your besetting sins? When you fail in this way, say to the individual with whom you have spoken, "Forgive me for damaging the reputation of another and pray for me that I may have a sweet and loving spirit." I guarantee that in a matter of weeks your tongue will be tamed.

Is the subtle sin of deception your downfall? Are you not quite truthful? When the lie crosses your lips, track it down and say to the one to whom you have lied, "Forgive me and pray for me that I may be truthful."

If you will deal with the wild things in your life like this in the presence of Jesus Christ, He will transform you at the center and make the point of your weakness the place of spiritual power. For this He has come and for this He is available.

> Make me a captive, Lord,
> And then I shall be free;
> Force me to render up my sword,
> And I shall conqueror be.
> I sink in life's alarms,
> When by myself I stand;
> Imprison me within Thine arms,
> And strong shall be my hand.
> George Matheson

WHAT JESUS SAYS ABOUT THE
EXCHANGED LIFE

*I am crucified with Christ: nevertheless I live . . . and
the life which I now live in the flesh I live by the faith of
the Son of God, who loved me, and gave himself for me.*

Galatians 2:20

MARK TWAIN, IN HIS IMAGINATIVE NOVEL, *"The Prince and the
Pauper,"* tells the story of two boys of the same age and identical in appearance—one a prince and heir to the royal throne,
the other an unfortunate and abused pauper.

By a coincidence, they are brought together and decide to
change places with each other, the prince putting on the rags
of the pauper and the pauper donning the royal garb of the
prince. The story continues by telling the adventures and experiences of each boy as he lives an exchanged life—each taking the place of the other.

This is an imaginative tale, but it serves as a springboard to
a solid and substantial fact far more radical and revolutionary
in its ramifications than the story of the Prince and the Pauper.
This fact is the exchanged life we can have in Jesus Christ,
who will take our place in the world and let us take His.

In this drama of life, the contrasts are even more extreme than in Mark Twain's story. The Prince before whom we stand is the Son of God, the Lord of Glory. His Kingdom is an everlasting Kingdom. His character is one of perfection, holiness, and love. We stand before Him less than paupers, for we are destitute and impoverished in spirit, transgressors of the law of His Kingdom, and rebels against His rule. Yet, He will exchange places with us.

The glad note of the gospel message in its essence is simply that God, in Christ, has taken our place, entered into all our suffering and sorrow, born with our willfulness and waywardness, and died our death for us. He bore all the consequences of our sin before the holiness of God. Then, having taken our place among men, He offers us His place before the Father —imputing to us His righteousness, sharing with us His life, lifting us to His eternal throne and the Father's infinite love.

Who can fully grasp the exultant witness of the Apostle Paul? "I am crucified with Christ: nevertheless I live; yet not I, but Christ liveth in me . . ." (*Gal. 2:20*). To the Apostle, this was the most glorious manifestation of God's grace in his experience. He had fought the cause of Christ. He had persecuted followers of the Way and had resisted the light. He had hated Jesus. Then, the living Lord appeared to him on the Damascus Road. He fell prostrate in the dust expecting the wrath of judgment, but instead he learned that this same Jesus had forgiven him and established him before God in the position of a son. Paul could express his wonder in no other way, ". . . who loved me and gave himself for me" (*Gal. 2:20*). I bring myself to Christ, my sinful self, my weakness, my failure, my unworthiness. I come as I am. He takes me and gives me Himself, all that He is and all that He has.

165

This amazing offer of an exchanged life involves more than the forgiveness of the past or the promise of the future. It also involves the present. It is not too difficult to trust the past to Christ or to rely on Him for eternal life in the future. But the present, with its discouragements and defeats, may prove more difficult. Yet the exchange which is offered us is a present exchange. These words of the text are in the present tense and one may paraphrase them: "Christ liveth in me: and the life which I now live in the flesh I live by the faith of the Son of God, who loved me, and gave himself for me" (*Gal. 2:20*). This is a contemporary thing.

Surely it is reasonable that God should offer His provision for today as well as for yesterday and tomorrow. In Jesus Christ, He not only saves us from the sins that are past, but from the sins that are present, not only from the circumstances which shall be with us tomorrow, but from the circumstances which confront us today. Dr. Thomas Chalmers, the Scottish preacher and theologian of the last century, writes, "The cross of Christ by the same mighty and decisive stroke whereby it moves the curse of sin away from us, surely moves the power of it from over us." Or this word of Scripture, "He that spared not his own Son, but delivered him up for us all, how shall he not with him also freely give us all things?" (*Romans* 8:32). God's love is of such a nature that He did not stop until He gave Himself to die our death. Will He, then, not help us to live His life? Christ offers to exchange lives with us today, to take our worry and weakness and give us His peace and power. He asks, "Would you not like to exchange places with Me? I will take you in your brokenness and defeat and move in to live My life through you." We turn to look at Him in wonder. "Lord, is this really possible? How may it be done?" He

166

seems to come closer. "You know that you cannot live the Christian life by yourself. '. . . Without me, ye can do nothing' " (*John 15:5*). Have you not found how helpless you are to be truly humble, loving, and spiritual? Even the full measure of your desire, determination, and self-discipline is not enough. He must live His life in you. It takes a little time for a Christian to learn that without Christ He can do nothing, yet it is a most important lesson to learn. Until we see our helplessness, there is little Christ can do to live His life in us, but when at last we face our inability and give Christ freedom to operate in us, He will exchange places with us.

An exchange always involves a movement in two directions. I give something and I receive something. In this case, I give myself to God and I receive from God the Spirit of Christ to live in me. The first step we might call surrender, commitment of life, or abandonment to God. The second step we might call appropriation, dependence, or trust in God.

First then, in an exchanged life we must give ourselves wholly and without reservation to God. Consider the way a potter shapes clay into a vessel. The part of the clay is simply to be pliable in the hands of the potter while his skillful fingers shape the clay into his design. The lump of clay cannot shape itself. It may lie in a clay-pit for a thousand years, but it will never be anything but a shapeless mass. In the hands of the potter, it soon becomes an object of utility and beauty.

As Christians, we are simply to place our lives in the hands of the Divine Potter and let Him mold us according to His pattern and purpose. There is only one question to be raised here. Do we really desire to be shaped in Christ's likeness? Do we really want His kind of life? If we do, let us put ourselves wholly in God's hands and authorize Him to shape us according to His plan and purpose.

To change the figure, an automobile should have only one driver. This is the only safe way to drive. If we want God to take our lives out on the highway of His will, then we must slip from behind the wheel and say, "Lord, take over." One reason our consecration has been so fruitless is that we have kept certain areas under our own control. We have kept a hand on the wheel—or at least a finger—and He does not have full liberty to direct and guide. Do you really want Christ to drive? Very well, turn the controls over to Him in an act of intelligent consecration. Take your hands completely off the wheel. Then relax, trust Him, respond to His direction. Don't be a back-seat driver. He is quite competent.

A Christian was seeking to explain the simplicity of a surrendered life to his friend, a physician in charge of a hospital. "Doctor," he said, "suppose a young man should say to you, 'I would like to have you cure my illness.' As you began to talk with him, you found that he was unwilling to tell you all the symptoms of his illness. Moreover, he refused to take the remedy that you offered but said, 'Very frankly, doctor, I will follow your advice in matters of which I approve, but in other matters I will make my own decisions.' Now what would you do with a case like that?" The doctor, somewhat bemused, said, "I would have nothing to do with a man like that. I could only help a patient who would put his whole case in my hands without reserve and who would implicitly follow my instructions." His friend answered, "That is what I mean by surrender. Will you put your life in the hands of Jesus Christ? Will you trust the Great Physician and follow His instructions?" The wise doctor said, "I will."

Does the thought of giving yourself to another bring fear to your heart? To whom are you giving your life? To God—to His Son, Jesus Christ! Are you taking such a big risk? Remember, He loves you and will continue to love you. His plan for your life is a perfect plan. His is the only One wise enough, good enough, and strong enough to give joy and victory. Why are you afraid to trust Jesus? But you say, "I have done that again and again and nothing ever happens. I have knelt by my bed more than once and said, 'Lord, take my life.' I really meant it, but I did not receive deliverance."

In order to bestow a gift upon another, it is necessary to believe that the person to whom it is given will take possession of it. In other words, giving our lives away to God involves an act of faith as well as dedication.

Let us imagine that you desire to give away some property. This may be highly imaginative, but at least we may use it for the sake of illustration. It is not possible to wrap up a house and lot and place them in the arms of a friend. You must make that transfer of property by an act of faith. A title deed is made out describing the property, designating the name of the, friend, and affixed with your signature. Your friend takes the title deed, places it in his pocket and gratefully walks away. Suppose that next day, you wonder, "Did I really give that property away? Does my friend know that it is now his?" So, you make out another title deed, rush to your friend and exclaim, "I want to give this property to you." "But," his friend says, "you gave it to me yesterday." "Yes, I know," you answer, "but I'm not sure if you really know that you have it. Here it is again." If this is repeated, your friend will question either your sanity or the genuineness of the gift. Yet here we are, giving our lives to Jesus Christ over and over again and never having assurance that we truly belong to Him.

This offer of my life is concluded by the acceptance of a fact—that my life now belongs to Christ. I rise from the transaction and view myself from a new aspect. I am no longer my own. I belong to God. I am His man, His woman. My time is no longer mine. I am His to use. I go to the office or the shop. It is not my business. It is not my shop. It is not my home. It is His. I now pray, "Lord, order this business as you desire. My talents and abilities are yours, to be used for your glory." I look at my family and friends. They are now God's too, held in a sacred trust for His love and purpose. I no longer own any property, nor do I have a bank account in my name alone. My substance is His. This is the foundation of Christian stewardship.

To give one tenth, the tithe of our income, to the church is more than generosity. It is a matter of integrity. All that we have belongs to God, and, as Christians, all that we have should be dedicated to Christ. Tithing does not mean that I give one tenth to God and keep nine tenths. Not at all. I give God one tenth for the work of His Kingdom, indicating that I recognize His ownership of the whole. This is simply the interest on His capital investment. The matter of stewardship of money is basic to spiritual success. If we are not trustworthy in small things, God cannot trust us with larger things. But once the transaction has been made, let us orient ourselves to the fact and know that it has been accepted. I am henceforth no longer my own. As the Apostle Paul said, "I am crucified with Christ . . ." and I myself am no longer living. Giving yourself away, then, is the first step.

The second step in the exchanged life is acceptance, my ap-

propriation of Jesus Christ for every need. The movement of
the exchange is in two directions. I give myself away and believe He takes me. Then I receive from Him what He offers me
of Himself. ". . . the life which I now live in the flesh, I live by
the faith of the Son of God . . ." (*Gal. 2:20*). This word may
be translated either "I am living in the Son of God" or "I
am living by the faithfulness of the Son of God." I prefer the
latter translation. It is not the quantity of faith that counts,
but its object, not the strength of one's faith, but the certainty
of God's faithfulness. I cannot live by my own fickle feeling,
but I can live by His faithfulness, trusting Him to live His life
in me.

Recently I had an appointment to meet some friends at a
football game. I was unavoidably delayed. As I was rushing up
the hill to the stadium, I heard the roar of the crowd, announc-
ing the kick-off. Someone touched my elbow as I pushed
toward the ticket window. I turned and saw a man with a
ticket in his hand. He smiled and said, "Would you like a ticket
to the game?" I hesitated, wondering if he was trying to
"scalp" the ticket or perhaps to sell it at a discount. He saw my
hesitation and volunteered, "Go ahead. I want to give it to
you. I can't make the game myself, and it will feel good to
know that you are enjoying it for me." I'm afraid I stood wide-
eyed in amazement. Something like this doesn't happen very
often. I was aware of a shadow of disappointment on the man's
face. He was hoping to see a response of real pleasure and
gratitude. Instead, he was looking at a strange, immobile person who was unwilling to take the ticket from him. When I
recognized the genuineness of his offer, I clasped his hand
and said warmly, "Thanks a lot. This is wonderful!" And we

both went on our way rejoicing. I had to accept that ticket by faith in another.

Jesus Christ offers to live His life in you, but He cannot do it until you trust Him enough to give Him the chance. He will exchange lives with you, but He must have your acceptance.

The same is true with love. In order to be received, love must be believed. You may be loved lavishly by another, but that love will not be yours until you believe that it is yours and receive it. Suppose a suitor proposes, saying, "Darling, I love you with all my heart." The girl queries, "Do you really love me?" "Yes" he avows, "I truly love you." "Truly, do you love me?" she keeps on asking, but what more can he do? To be known, love must be trusted and received.

God loves you. Jesus Christ loves you. He gave Himself for you. God loves every creature in His universe, but His love cannot be known until His creature—man, for whom He gave Himself—believes and receives the gift of His love. When this truth is accepted and appropriated, the exchanged life begins.

WHAT JESUS SAYS ABOUT HIS
HOME IN THE HEART

*That he would grant you, according to the riches of
his glory, to be strengthened with might by his Spirit
in the inner man; that Christ may dwell in your
hearts by faith. . . .*

Ephesians 3:16,17

In Paul's Epistle to the Ephesians, we find these words:
"That he would grant you, according to the riches of his glory,
to be strengthened with might by his Spirit in the inner man;
that Christ may dwell in your hearts by faith . . . ," or, as
another has translated, "That Christ may settle down and be
at home in your hearts by faith."

Without question, one of the most remarkable Christian
doctrines is that Jesus Christ Himself, through the presence
of the Holy Spirit, will actually enter a heart, settle down
there, and be at home. Christ will make the human heart His
abode.

Our Lord said to His disciples, ". . . If a man loves me, he
will keep my word, and my Father will love him, and we will

come to him and make our home with him" (*John 14:23, RSV*).
It was difficult for them to understand what He was saying.
How was it possible for Him to make His abode with them in
this sense?

It is interesting that our Lord used the same word here
that He gave them in the fourteenth chapter of John. ". . .
I go and prepare a place for you . . . that where I am, you
may be also" (*John 14:3 RSV*). Our Lord was promising His
disciples that, just as He was going to heaven to prepare a
place for them and would welcome them one day, it was possible for them now to prepare a place for Him in their hearts.
He would come and make His home with them within. They
could not understand this. How could it be? Then came Pentecost and the Spirit of the living Christ was given to the
church and they knew what He meant. God did not dwell in
Herod's temple in Jerusalem nor in a temple made with
hands. Through the gift of the Holy Spirit, God would dwell
in human personality. The body of the believer would be the
temple of the living God, and the human heart would be the
home of Jesus Christ.

There is a picture in the gospels of a home where our Lord
was always welcome and where He often returned with delight. It was the home of Mary and Martha and their brother
Lazarus, just outside Jerusalem. Often, on His way to the great
city, our Lord went to this home and found rest and refresh-
ment from the weary journey. Or, returning from Jerusalem
after having spent a day beset with antagonism, He sought
refuge and companionship in the home of His friends. How
grateful He must have been for the freedom and the love
which they offered Him in that home! There He was welcomed and royally received. But think also what our Lord

must have brought into that home when He came. He brought His own radiant presence, His peace and His power. He promised them, ". . . if thou wouldest believe, thou shouldest see the glory of God" (*John 11:40*). They saw the glory of God in the raising of Lazarus to life at Christ's spoken word.

This same Lord is with us. These hearts of ours may be just as truly a home for Jesus Christ as the house in which Mary, Martha, and Lazarus dwelt so long ago. We think of our own bodies as a structure—the walls, flesh and blood, the door, the human will. If Jesus Christ is welcomed there, He will settle down and be at home.

I would like to tell you how I have come to think of Christ dwelling in my heart. I will use the first person singular only to make it more vivid. There have been two major events in my life. One was the step of marriage. I recall my first reactions to the matter of matrimony. When I was single, many said to me, "You ought to marry. Your life would be more complete." I would agree with them in theory. But when I thought of my independence in contrast to some of the obligations and responsibilities of matrimony, I was rather hesitant. The longer one waits, the more cautious one becomes. Then one day, a very charming young lady walked across my path, and immediately I became interested in her. I came to know her better, and soon, in spite of myself, all my hesitancy and caution regarding married life were gone. I could not think of anything I wanted to do more than to spend my life with her. We were married, and I have never regretted that step. She was the one for me. I have found in that relationship satisfaction, joy, and real delight.

The other major event was receiving Jesus Christ as my Lord and Saviour. To be frank, I was very cautious about this

also. I treasured my independence. I liked to order my life the way I pleased, and I felt that Jesus Christ would have a narrowing and confining influence. If He really were alive, as others said, and if I committed myself to Him unreservedly, He might direct me into paths I did not desire to enter. But God in His infinite mercy gave me a good look at Christ. He attracted me. He won me until I desired Him and no longer desired my own independence. One evening I invited Him into my heart. What an entrance He made! It was not a spectacular, emotional thing, but very real. Something happened at the very center of my life. He came into the darkness of my heart and turned on the light. He built a fire on the hearth and banished the chill. He started music where there had been stillness, and He filled the emptiness with His own loving, wonderful fellowship. I have never regretted opening the door to Christ and I never will—not into eternity!

This, of course, is the first step in making the heart Christ's home. He has said, "Behold, I stand at the door, and knock: if any man hear my voice, and open the door, I will come in to him, and will sup with him, and he with me" (*Rev. 3:20*). If you are interested in making your life an abode of the living God, let me encourage you to invite Christ into your heart. He will surely come.

In the joy of this new-found relationship, I said to Him, "Lord, I want this heart of mine to be Yours. I want to have You settle down here and be perfectly at home. Everything I have belongs to You. Let me show You around and introduce You to the various features of the home that You may be more comfortable and that we may have fuller fellowship together." He was very gracious and seemed glad to come.

The first room was the study—the library. In my home this room of the mind is a very small room with very thick walls, but it is a very important room. In a sense, it is the control-room of the house. He entered with me and looked around at the books in the bookcase, the magazines upon the table, the pictures on the wall. As I followed His gaze I became uncomfortable. Strangely enough, I had not felt self-conscious about this before, but now that He was there looking at these things I was embarrassed. Some books were there that His eyes were too pure to behold. There was a lot of trash and literature on the table that a Christian had no business to read, and as for the pictures on the wall—the imaginations and thoughts of the mind—some of these were shameful. I turned to Him and said, "Master, I known that this room needs radical alterations. Will You help me make it what it ought to be and bring every thought into captivity to Thee?" "Surely!" He said. "Gladly I will help you. That is one reason I am here. First of all, take all the things that you are reading and looking at which are not helpful, pure, good, and true and throw them out. Now put on the empty shelves the Books of the Bible. Fill the library with Scripture and 'meditate therein day and night' (*Joshua 1:8*). As for the pictures on the wall, you will have difficulty controlling these images, but here is an aid." He gave me a full-sized portrait of Himself. "Hang this centrally," He said, "on the wall of the mind." I did and I have discovered through the years that when my attention is centered upon Christ Himself, His purity and power cause impure imaginations to retreat. So He has helped me to bring my thoughts into captivity. May I suggest to you if you have difficulty with this little room of the mind, that you bring Christ in there. Fill

your thoughts with the truths of the Bible and recognize the presence of the Master.

From the study we went into the dining room, the room of appetites and desires. This was a very large room in my house. I spent a good deal of time here and much effort in satisfying my wants. I said to Him, "This is a very commodious room, and I am quite sure You will be pleased with what we serve." He seated Himself at the table with me and asked, "What is on the menu for dinner?" "Well," I said, "my favorite dishes, old bones, corn husks, sour garbage, leeks, onions, and garlic right out of Egypt." These were the things I liked—worldly fare. I suppose there was nothing wrong in any particular item, but it was not the food that should satisfy a real Christian. When the food was placed before Him, He said nothing, but I observed that He did not eat it. I said to Him, somewhat disturbed, "Master, You don't care for this food? What is the trouble?" He answered, "I have meat to eat that ye know not of. . . . My meat is to do the will of him that sent me . . ." (*John 4:32, 34*). He looked at me again. "If you want food that really satisfies, seek the will of the Father, not your own pleasures, not your own desires, not your own satisfaction, but seek to please Me. That food will satisfy you." There about the table, He gave me a taste of the joy of doing God's will. What flavor! What nourishment and vitality it gives to the soul! There is no food like it in all the world. It alone satisfies. Everything else is dissatisfying in the end.

If Christ is in your heart, what kind of food are you serving Him? What kind of food are you eating yourself? Are you living selfishly? Or are you choosing God's will for your meat and your drink?

From the dining-room we walked into the drawing-room.

This room was intimate and comfortable. I liked it. It had a fireplace, upholstered chairs, a sofa, and a quiet atmosphere. He seemed pleased with it. He said, "This is indeed a delightful room. Let us come here often. It is secluded and quiet, and we can fellowship together." Well, naturally, as a young Christian I was thrilled. I could not think of anything I would rather do than have a few minutes apart with Christ in intimate fellowship. He promised "I will be here early every morning. Meet Me here, and we will start the day together." So, morning after morning, I would come downstairs to the drawing-room—or withdrawing-room as I liked to think of it. He would take a Book of the Bible from the bookcase. We would open it and read together. He would tell me of its richness and unfold to me its truths. My heart warmed as He revealed the love and the grace He had toward me. These were wonderful hours.

Little by little, under the pressure of many responsibilities, this time began to be shortened. Why, I don't know, but I thought I was too busy to spend time with Christ. This was not intentional, you understand. It just happened that way. Finally, not only was the time shortened, but I began to miss a day now and then. Perhaps it was examination time at the University. Perhaps it was some other urgent emergency. I would miss it two days in a row and oftentimes more. I remember one morning when I was rushing downstairs, eager to be on my way, that I passed the drawing room and noticed that the door was ajar. Looking in, I saw a fire in the fireplace and the Master sitting there. Suddenly in dismay I thought to myself, "He is my Guest. I invited Him into my heart! He has come and yet I am neglecting Him." With downcast glance, I said, "Blessed Master, forgive me. Have You been here all these mornings?" "Yes," He said, "I told you I would be here every morning to meet with you." Then I was even more ashamed. He had been faithful in spite of my faithlessness. I asked His forgiveness, and He readily forgave me as He does when we are truly penitent.

Then He told me, "The trouble is that you have been thinking of the quiet time, of Bible study and prayer as factors for your own spiritual progress. You have forgotten that this hour means something to Me also. Remember, I love you. I have redeemed you at great cost. I desire your fellowship. Even if you cannot keep the quiet time for your own sake, do it for Mine." The truth that Christ desires my companionship, that He wants me to be with Him and waits for me, has done more to transform my quiet time with God than any other single factor. Don't let Christ wait alone in the drawing room of your heart, but every day find time, when, with your Bible and in prayer, you may have fellowship with Him.

Before long, He asked, "Do you have a workshop in your home?" Down in the basement of the home of my heart, I had a workbench and some equipment, but I was not doing much with it. Once in a while I would go down and fuss around with a few little gadgets, but I wasn't producing anything substantial. I led Him down there. He looked over the workbench and what little talents and skills I had. He said, "Well, this is quite well furnished. What are you producing with your life for the Kingdom of God?" He looked at one or two little toys that I had thrown together on the bench. He held one up to me and said, "Are these little toys all that you are producing in your Christian life?" "Well," I said, "Lord, that is the best I can do. I know it isn't much, and I really want to do more, but, after all, I don't seem to have strength or skill to do more."

"Would you like to do better?" He asked. "Certainly," I replied. "All right. Let me have your hands. Now relax in Me and let My Spirit work through you. I know that you are clumsy and awkward, but the Holy Spirit is the Master Workman, and if He controls your hands and your heart, He will work through you." Stepping around behind me and putting His great, strong hands under mine, holding the tools in His skilled fingers, He began to work through me. The more I relaxed and trusted Him, the more He was able to do with my life.

There is much more that I must learn, and I am far from satisfied with the products that are being turned out, but I do know that whatever has been produced for God has been through His strength and the working of His Spirit.

Do not become discouraged because you cannot do much for God. Ability is not the fundamental question; it is our availability. Upon whom are we relying? Let us give our talents to God. He will do things with them that will surprise us.

He asked me if I had a playroom. I was hoping He would not ask me about this. There were certain associations and friendships, activities, and amusements that I wanted to keep for myself. I did not think Christ would enjoy them or approve of them, so I evaded the question. One evening when I was leaving to join some college companions, He stopped me with a glance. "Are you going out this evening?" I replied, "Yes." "Good," He said, "I would like to go with you." "Oh," I answered rather awkwardly. "I don't think, Lord Jesus, that You would really want to go with me. Let's go out tomorrow night. Tomorrow night we will go to prayer meeting, but tonight I have another appointment." "I'm sorry," He said, "I thought that when I came into your home, we were going to

do everything together, to be partners. I want you to know
that I am willing to go with you." "Well," I mumbled, slipping
out the door, "we will go some place tomorrow night." That
evening I spent some miserable hours. I felt wretched. What
kind of a friend was I to Christ when I was deliberately leaving Him out of my associations, doing things and going places
that I knew very well He would not enjoy? When I returned
that evening, there was a light in His room, and I went up to
talk it over with Him. I said, "Lord, I have learned my lesson.
I cannot have a good time without You. We will do everything
together." Then we went down into the rumpus room of the
house and He transformed it. He brought new friends into
my life, new satisfactions, new and lasting joys. Laughter and
music have been ringing through the house ever since.

There is just one more matter that I might share with you.
One day I found Him waiting for me at the door. There was an
arresting look in His eye, and He said to me as I entered,
"There is a peculiar odor in the house. Something is dead
around here. It's upstairs. I'm sure it is in the hall-closet." As
soon as He said the words, I knew what He was talking about.
Yes, there was a small hall-closet up there on the landing, just
a few feet square. In that closet, behind lock and key, I had
one or two little personal things that I did not want Christ to
see. I knew they were dead and rotting things, and I wanted
them so for myself that I was afraid to admit they were there.
I went up with Him, and as we mounted the stairs, the odor
became stronger and stronger. He pointed to the door and
said, "It's in there!—some dead thing!" I was angry. That's the
only way I can put it. I had given Him access to the library,
the dining-room, the drawing-room, the workshop, the rumpus room, and now He was asking me about a little two-by-

four closet. I said inwardly, "This is too much. I am not going to give Him the key." "Well," He said, reading my thoughts, "If you think I'm going to stay up here on the second floor with this odor, you are mistaken. I will go out on the porch. I'm certainly not going to put up with that." I saw Him start down the stairs. My resistance collapsed. When one comes to know and love Christ, the worst thing that can happen is to sense His companionship retreating. I had to surrender. "I'll give You the key," I said sadly, "but You will have to open up the closet and clean it out. I haven't the strength to do it." "I know," He said, "I know. Just give me the key. Just authorize Me to take care of that closet and I will." So, with trembling fingers, I passed the key over to Him. He took it from my hand, walked over to the door, opened it, entered it, took out all the putrifying stuff that was rotting there, and threw it away. Then He cleaned the closet, painted it, and fixed it up. It was done in a moment's time. Oh, what victory and release to have that dead thing out of my life!

Then a thought came to me. I said to myself. "I have been trying to keep this heart of mine clean for Christ. I start on one room, and no sooner have I cleaned it than another room is dirty. I begin in the second room, and the first room becomes dusty again. I am tired and weary seeking to have a clean heart and an obedient life. I am just not up to it!" So I ventured this question. "Lord, is there any chance that You would take over the management of the whole house and operate it for me as You did that closet? Would You take the responsibility to keep my life what it ought to be?" His face lighted up as He replied, "Certainly, that is what I want to do. You cannot be a victorious Christian in your own strength. That is impossible. Let Me do it through you and for you. That is the way. But," He added slowly, "I am not owner of this house. I am just a guest. I have no authority to proceed since the property is not mine." I saw it in a minute and, dropping to my knees, I said, "Lord, You have been a guest and I have been the host. From now on I am going to be the servant. You are going to be the Lord." Running as fast as I could to the strong box, I took out the title deed to the house describing its properties, assets, and liabilities. Then, returning to Him, I eagerly signed it over to Him alone for time and eternity. "Here," I said, "Here it is, all that I am and have forever. Now You run the house. I'll just remain with You as a servant and friend."

He has been faithful to me as Lord of my life. Things are different since Jesus Christ has settled down and made His home in my heart.

> Oh, the bitter pain and sorrow
> That a time could ever be
> When I proudly said to Jesus—
> "All of self, and none of thee."
>
> Yet He found me; I beheld Him
> Bleeding on th' accursed tree;
> And my wistful heart said faintly,
> "Some of self and some of Thee."
>
> Day by day His tender mercy
> Healing, helping, full and free,
> Brought me lower, while I whispered—
> "Less of self, and more of Thee!"

Higher than the highest heaven,
Deeper than the deepest sea,
Lord, Thy love at last has conquered;
"None of self and ALL of Thee!"